Edward Frossard

Catalogue of the numismatic collection of William Poillon

Part 1

Edward Frossard

Catalogue of the numismatic collection of William Poillon
Part 1

ISBN/EAN: 9783742818850

Manufactured in Europe, USA, Canada, Australia, Japa

Cover: Foto ©Thomas Meinert / pixelio.de

Manufactured and distributed by brebook publishing software
(www.brebook.com)

Edward Frossard

Catalogue of the numismatic collection of William Poillon

The
POILLON COLLECTION.
Part I.

Sale of

Coins, Medals and Books.

December 12–15, 1883.

CATALOGUE

OF THE

Numismatic Collection

Of WILLIAM POILLON, Esq., of New York.

PART I.

UNITED STATES COINS, SILVER AND COPPER,

Colonial Coins, Pattern Pieces,

Washington Medals, Army and Navy Medals, Masonic Medals,
Foreign Coins, a Superb Collection of

AMERICAN STORE CARDS,

COLONIAL AND CONTINENTAL PAPER MONEY,

United States Fractional Currency, Confederate Bonds and Notes,

Coin Catalogues,

A VERY COMPLETE NUMISMATIC LIBRARY,

Etc., Etc., Etc.

———

TO BE SOLD AT AUCTION,

On DECEMBER 12, 13, 14, 15, 1888,

By Messrs. BANGS & CO.,

739 & 741 Broadway, New York.

Each Sale begins at Two o'clock in the Afternoon.

Catalogue by ED. FROSSARD,

IRVINGTON ON HUDSON, NEW YORK.

THIRTY-THIRD SALE.

- •••

BOSTON:
T. R. MARVIN & SON, NUMISMATIC PRINTERS.
1888.

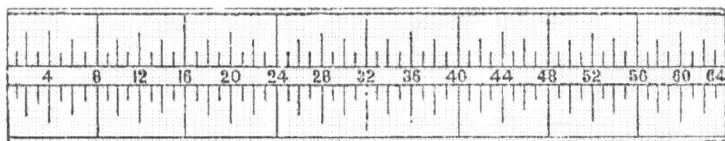

AMERICAN COIN SCALE.

NOTE. — A special edition of that Catalogue comprising the Numismatic Library is issued. Copies can be had, on application, from Messrs. Bangs & Co., or the undersigned. 25 copies of the entire Catalogue, thick paper, can be obtained immediately after the Sale, neatly priced, at one dollar each.

ED. FROSSARD, Irvington, N. Y.

ORDER OF SALE.

WEDNESDAY, December 12. Numbers 1 to 630, inclusive.

THURSDAY, December 13, Numbers 631 to 1260, inclusive.

FRIDAY, December 14, Numbers 1261 to 1892, inclusive.

SATURDAY, December 15, Numbers 1893 to the end.

CATALOGUE.

FOREIGN COPPER COINS.

1 Antigua. 1836. Farthing: fine.

2 Australia. Halfpenny tokens. Includes the "Montpelier
Retreat Inn" and "Baby Linen Warehouse." All very
fine and scarce. 17. 4 pieces

3 Austria. 1760 to recent issues. Large and small. Aver.
very good. 60 pieces.

4 1807 Francis. 30 kreutzer, necessity. Fine. 22.

5 1852 Imperio Austriaco. 10 centesimi. Uncir. 16.

6 Bahama. 1806. Halfpenny. Very fine: scarce.

7 Barbadoes. 1788. Penny. Negro crowned and pineapple;
1792, halfpenny, rev., Neptune. Very good. 2 pieces

8 Moses Tolando; token. "Freedom without Slavery."
Fine, but pierced. 18.

9 Bermuda. 1793. Halfpenny. Good: scarce.

10 Belgium. Includes "1 kreutzer, Zelandia, 1788"; several
nickel. Fair to fine. 22 pieces.

11 1750–1795 Ad usum Belgii, etc.; 4 with bust of Maria
Theresa. Very fine. 14 to 16. 6 pieces.

12 Brazil. 1747–1820. 10 to 80 reis. Several counterstamped. Average very good. 16 to 20. 14 pieces.

13 Another lot. Fair to good: nearly all large. 17 pieces.

14 Canada. Collection of Provincial coins and tokens, comprising a number of very scarce issues. Many varieties:
some duplicates. Aver. condition v. good. 165 pieces.

15 Ships, Colonies & Commerce, with part of the rev. struck
over the ship. Reverse Blank. Fine; and a desirable
oddity.

16 Ceylon. 1802, $\frac{1}{192}$ of a dollar, fine: 1815 half, and two stivers, fair and good. 11 to 20.   3 pieces

17 China. Temple medal. Dragons on each side : inscription on reverse. Brass : good and rare. 34.

18 Another. Eagle above : dragons on the side and below the usual square hole in centre. Rev. Inscription. Brass : very fine and rare. 30.

19 Another. Mandarin and flower. Brass : fine. 18.

20 Inscription on one side. Rev. Blank. Brass : fine and rare. 21 to 26.   3 pieces

21 Cash. Copper and brass. Many varieties of the usual type. Average very good. 10 to 22.   89 pieces

22 Chinese coins fastened to pasteboard, giving dates of the several coinages. Fine.   12 pieces

23 Denmark. 2, 1, and ½ skilling. Uncirculated set. 10 to 17.   3 pieces

24 Dominica (2). Demerary and Essequebo, Dutch Indies. 1810–1857. All fine.   13 pieces

25 East India (British) 1803–1862 pic, ¼ and ½ anna. 10 and 20 cash, ¼, ½, and 1 cent, etc. Average fine. 10 to 18.   30 pieces

26 England. Charles I. Farthing or " Black money " ; Charles II, 1672 and '73, farthings. Fair to good. 3 pcs

27 William and Mary, 1694 ; William III. 1697. Half pennies and farthings. Poor to good.   4 pieces

28 William and Mary. Pattern farthing. One head on each side. Poor : rare.

29 Anne. Farthing. The reverse has been filed flat and engraved with the letters *T. G.* in a wreath, as a love token. Nicked on edge : genuine.

30 George III. 1797. Twopence. Fine : a little nicked. 26.

31 The same. 1797. Penny : 2d coinage. Uncirculated.

32 The same. 1799. Halfpenny and farthing. Very fine and uncirculated.   2 pieces

33 George IV. 1826. Halfpenny. Nearly bright red : uncir.

34 George I. 1717, to Victoria, 1873. Pence, halfpence and farthings. No duplicates. Fair to uncirculated ; average condition fine.   74 pieces

35 1825–'52. Half, ⅓ and ¼ farthing. Fine.   5 pieces

36 Victoria. Pattern ¼ and ⅛ sovereign, crown, pence, half-pence, 1, ½, ¼, ⅛, and 1⁄16 farthing. Copper and brass. One pierced : an extremely fine lot, containing a number of so-called gold and silver centres.   22 pieces

37 Spade guinea, one, and half guinea; also medallions of George IV and Victoria. Brass; three-pierced. Average very good. 14 pieces

38 Tokens. Birmingham. 1812. Threepence. Largest English token. Copper; fine and rare. 2s.

39 Tradesmen tokens. Penny size, 1788-1815. All different and fine. 6 pieces

40 Portrait tokens. Halfpenny size. John of Gaunt. T Hardy, Earl Howe, Isaac Newton. Prince and Princess of Wales. Good to bright red. 7 pieces

41 Tradesmen halfpenny tokens. 1789-1812. A few bright red, several quite scarce, average condition very good. 28 pieces

42 Town tokens, halfpenny size. Bath. Berwick. Bungay. Chichester. Coventry (Lady Godiva). Falmouth. Hull. Leeds. Leek. Liverpool. London. Macclesfield. Newgate. Norwich. Rochdale. Sheffield. Shire Hall, Southampton. South Shields. Average good or v. good, one pierced. 23 pieces

43 Farthing tokens. Copper and brass, one pierced. Very good to fine. 10 pieces

44 Gambling tokens. Copper, brass and w. m. 12 pieces

45 Holland. 1607-1794. Includes Campen, Utrecht, Zeelandia, Overyssel, Groningen, Surinam, etc. An extremely fine lot, containing several rarities. 12 to 18. 26 pieces

46 Copper jetons. Philip IV and VI. Charles II and V4, etc. Fair to fine. 14 to 19. 5 pieces

47 Ionian Islands. 1819 and 1862. Farthing and half farthing. Fine; the former very scarce. 2 pieces

48 France. Louis XIII to the present Republic. Average condition very good, several very fine; few of any duplicates. 86 pieces

49 Napoleon I. 1815. Five francs; copper. Very fine.

50 Napoleon II. Half franc and 5 centimes; same. Copper. fine. 2 pieces

51 Monneron token. 1792. Very fine. 2s. 2 pieces

52 Siege coins. Mayence, 1793, 2 sous; Antwerp, 10 cents, L. and N. varieties, and 5 cents N. Fine and rather fine. 5 pieces

53 Cayenne. (Cayenne) crowned. 1788 etc., several uncommon. unstamped. Fair lot. 14. 15 pieces

54 Collection of French medalets, nearly all with bust: Napoleon I and family, Napoleon III, French celebrities, National events, etc.; quite a number with loops soldered on edge; also a few early copper jetons. Average condition very fine, many perfectly uncir., and all different. Cop., brass, and silvered. 8 to 20. 59 pcs

55 **Greece.** 1828–1857. 2, 5, and 10 lepta. Good and fine.
3 pieces

56 **Germany.** Collection of copper coins of the various States, many old dates of unusual types and rare. Average condition fine. 165 pieces

57 **Gibraltar.** 1810 and 1820. 1 and 2 quartos. Good and fine. 3 pieces

58 **Guernsey.** 1830 and 1834. 1, 4, and 8 doubles. Fine to uncirculated. 3 pieces

59 **Haiti.** 1829–1863. Good to fine. 10 to 20. 12 pieces

60 **Hong Kong.** 1863 and 1866. Mills and cent. Fine and uncirculated. 3 pieces

61 **Hungary.** 1848 and 1849. Egy and harom Krajczar, and another. Fine. 3 pieces

62 **Italy.** Collection of copper coins of the various States, including Papal, Venice, Sicily, etc. Many types and varieties; average large and fine. 9 to 24. 67 pieces

63 **Ireland.** Elizabeth, 1601 penny; Charles I, Harrington farthings. Fair. 3 pieces

64 Charles II. 1680. Halfpenny. Good. 17.

65 James II. Gun money. 1689–1690. Crown, half (3), and shillings, varieties of issue; nearly all fine. 10 pcs

66 William and Mary. 1693. Halfpenny: Wood's halfpennies, 1723 and '24. Fair to good. 4 pieces

67 George II, 1743, halfpenny; 1760, h'fpenny and farthing; George III, 1766 and 1782, halfpennies. Fair to good.
5 pieces

68 1789 Cronebane halfpenny. Bright red; scarce.

69 1792–1804. Halfpenny tokens. Poor to very good. 5 pcs.

70 1805–1823. George III and IV. Pennies, halfpennies, and farthings. Fair to very fine. 10 pieces

71 Halfpenny token. HOLMES IRISH CUTLERY, Dublin. Very fine; rare.

72 Belfast Church token. " The gospel is preached," etc. Fine; pierced.

73 Farthing tokens. Belfast, Cork, Dublin, Galway, and Longford. Good to fine. 13 pieces

74 Isle of Man. 1733, '68, '86, '98, 1811, 13, 31, and 39. Pennies, halfpence, and farthings; also, Falkner's Bazaar, Athole Street, Douglass, farthing token. Very fair to fine; a scarce lot. 14 pieces

75 Japan. Tempo; two, one, half sen, rin. Uncirculated. 4 pieces

76 Jamaica. M. Howard and William Smith. Penny and halfpenny tokens. Good. 2 pieces

77 Jersey. 1851, 1/13 shilling, good; 1858, 1/26 and 1/52 shilling, uncirculated. 5 pieces

78 Liberia. 1847. One and two cents. Very good. 2 pes

79 Luxembourg. 1860. 10 centimes. Fine. 2 pieces.

80 Maranhao. M and XX counterstamped on 40 reis of Brazil, 1827. Fine and rare. 54.

81 Malta. Emanuel de Rohan. G. M. (5), and Raymond de Perellos. Average good, and all very scarce. 8 pes

82 Mexico. Includes Chihuahua, Jalisco, Sinaloa, and several tokens. Average condition very good, and a rare lot. 27 pieces

83 Miscellaneous. A number fine, culled from preceding lots; others poor, pierced, etc. Includes also brass jeton, counterfeit coins, a South American brass button, etc. 45 pieces

84 Monaco. Honoré V. 1837 and '38. 5 and 10 centimes. Fine. 2 pieces

85 Persia. Lion crowned, date 1869 in exergue; another with half moon over elephant. Thick; fine. 7 and 12. 2 pieces

86 Poland. John Casimir, Augustus, 1828, 1831, and 1841. 3 grosze. One bright red, balance fair. 6 pieces

87 Portugal. 1752-1850. 3, 5, 10, 20, XX, 40, and 80 reis; includes Madeira and St. Thomas. Two pierced; good to fine. 16 to 24. 12 pieces

88 Portuguese Africa. 1860, macuta; 1861, half macuta. Fine and uncirculated. 24. 2 pieces

89 Russia. 1731, 35, 67, 70, 77, 89, 90, and 94. 1 to 5 kopeks. Several types; good to fine. 14 to 26. 8 pes

90 1802 and '03. 2 and 5 kopeks. Fine. 22 and 25. 2 pes

91 1811-14. 1 and 2 kopeks. Fair to fine. 5 pieces.

92 1882 and 86. 1, 5, and 10 kopeks, the latter size 28. Fine. 4 pieces

93 1810-1874. 1/4, 1, 2, 3, and 5 kopeks, etc. A fine lot. 27 pieces

94 **Siberia.** 1770 and '75. 5 and 10 kopecs. ~~Fine and~~ rare.
22 and 28. 2 pieces

95 **Scotland.** Mary. 1555. Hard-head or lion. M crowned
and lion crowned. Fine and rare. 10.

96 **Charles I.** 1629–1642. Twopence, or " turners : "
Charles II, bawbee ; William and Mary, twopence.
All very scarce, but average condition barely fair.
7 pieces

97 **Tradesmen** halfpenny and farthing tokens. Culross,
Edinburgh, Glasgow. Inverness, Montrose, Perth ; also
Glasgow omnibus token for 2 pence One pierced :
average very good. 13 pieces

98 **Siam.** Pewter money with square hole in centre, similar
to the Chinese cash. String of about 300 pcs. The lot.

99 **Spain.** 1603–1870. Includes 4 cuartos Barcelona 1810,
and 6 cuartos Cataluna 1838. Good and sc. lot. 30 pcs

100 **St. Helena.** 1821. Halfpenny. Uncirculated.

101 **Sweden.** 1683–1864. Includes several scarce tokens,
also a penny of Riga, 1554. Average very good. 9 to
24. 43 pieces

102 **1835–'49.** One-sixth, one-third, two-thirds, 1, 2, and 4
skilling banco. Fine to uncir. 10 to 24. 9 pieces

103 **Charles XII.** 1715–'19. Copper dalers. A very fine
and complete set. 10 pieces

104 **Duplicates.** 9 varieties. Average very good. 18 pieces

105 **Switzerland.** Principally nickel : a few Cantonal. 30 ps

106 **South America.** Buenos Ayres. 1823–'40. Decimo,
real, etc. Very good and sc. 14 to 16. 4 pieces

107 **1830** Banco Nacional, Buenos Ayres. 10 decim. Fine ,
rare. 18.

108 **Argentine** Confederation. 1854. 2 and 4 centavos. Very
fine. 18 and 22. 2 pieces

109 **Buenos Ayres** Coliseum. Entrance token : counterstamped. 20.

110 **1835–'71.** Argentine Confed., Chili, Guatemala, New
Granada. Uruguay, Venezuela, etc. A few nickel :
average condition very good. 12 to 24. 36 pieces

111 **Chili.** 1868. Medio decimo. Brilliant proof. 10.

112 **Honduras.** 1833 and '53. Provisional two reales. Fair
and good, one pierced. 16 to 18. 2 pieces

113 **Turkey** also Tripoli and Tunis. Very fine ; several of
the largest size. 17 pieces

FOREIGN COINS—SILVER

114 Austria. 1628–1692. Ferdinand II and Leopold, bigmouth. 8 and 15 kreutzer. Fair to fine. 5 pieces

115 Maria Theresa. 1780. Levant crown. Uncirculated.

116 Duplicate of last number. Very fine.

117 1797–1868 5, 6, 10, 20 kreutzer, half florin, etc. Very fine. 8 pieces

118 Francis Joseph 1857. Vereinsthaler. Uncirculated.

119 Bohemia. 1619. 20 kreutzer. Crowned lion and crown. Varieties; uncirculated. 20. 2 pieces

120 Frederic. 1620. Crowned bust. Rev. Arms. Fine. 20.

121 Belgium. 1722. Gulden. Liberty with cap. Rev. Arms. Rude, but fine.

122 Leopold I 1840 and 1844. 2 and 1 francs; also 1868. 1 franc. Very good. 3 pieces

123 Leopold II. 1869. 5 francs. Uncirculated.

124 The same. 1866 and '67. 50 centimes, 1 and 2 francs. Fine and uncirculated. 3 pieces

125 Brazil. 1751. 600 reis. Rio Janeiro mint. Very good. 20.

126 Charles IV dollar, counterstamped on each side with Brazilian arms. Very good.

127 1820. 960 and 320 reis (dollar and one-third dollar). Fine. 2 pieces

128 1868. 2,000 reis, new coinage, or dollar. Uncirculated.

129 1861 and '65. 1,000 reis. Uncirculated. 2 pieces

130 1850, '64, and '68. 500 reis; also 1865, 100 reis. One with bust of Pedro II. Very fine or uncirculated. 4 pieces

131 Canada. 1858. 20, 10, and 5 cents. Very good and fine. 3 pieces

132 1870. 50, 25, 10, and 5 cents. Uncirculated. 4 pieces

133 1871. 50, 25, 10, and 5 cents. Very fine or uncirculated. 4 pieces

134 1871. 50, 10 (2), and 5 cents. Very fine or uncirculated. 4 pieces

135 Chili. 1868. Un peso, or dollar. Arms, supported by 2 plumes and angle with shield. Uncirculated.

136 1848 Un peso. Same type as last. Very fine.

137 1853–70. ½ and ¼ decimos. 20 cents. Good or uncirculated. 4 pieces

138 Denmark. Carolus Gustavus. Christian IV. Frederic
III, etc. Base silver coins. Fair to fine. 10 to 18.
5 pieces

139 Christian IV, 1630; Frederic III, 1665: Frederic IV,
1704. 8 and 16 skilling; fine silver. Fine. 3 pieces

140 Christian V. 1672. Two marks, struck for Norway.
Fine. 20.

141 1701-1856. 2 to 16 skilling; also, 20 cents, 2 and 10
skilling. Dansk America. Very good, several base.
18 pieces.

142 Christian VII. 1795. Crown. Bust and crowned shield.
Very good.

143 Christian VIII. 1846. Crown. Bust and arms supported
by naked men. Fine.

144 England. Henry VIII. Groat, 2nd coinage. Crowned
bust to right; *m. m.* a lily. Fine and scarce.

145 The same. Groat, 3rd coinage. Crowned bust, nearly
facing; *m. m.* a lily. Very good, rare.

146 The same. Groat, 4th coinage. York mint. Very good
and scarce.

147 The same. Groat, 5th coinage. Bristol mint. *m. m.* a lily.
Good for this very rare issue.

148 Elizabeth. 1561. Sixpence, hammered money; fine, but
pierced. Also, Henry III, penny: fair. James I,
1607, sixpence: fair. 3 pieces

149 The same. 1580. Sixpence, hammered money; *m. m.*
Knight Templar's cross. Fine.

150 Charles II. Maundy set, without date. I, II, III, and
IIII behind the head. Uncirculated and scarce. 4 pcs

151 The same. 1672-'84. One to fourpence, Maundy.
Very fine or uncirculated. 4 pieces

152 James II. 1685. Shilling. Four shields crowned on
reverse. Good; rare.

153 The same. 1686 and '87. One to fourpence, Maundy,
by *Roettier.* Crowned numerals on reverse. Uncirculated and rare. 4 pieces

154 William and Mary. 1691 Half-crown. Monogram in
angles on rev. Very good.

155 The same. 1692. Crown; same type as last number.
Nearly fine.

156 The same. 1693. Shilling and sixpence. Same type.
Very good. 2 pieces

157 The same. 1689 and '90. Maundy set. Rev. Numerals
crowned. Very fine. 4 pieces

158 William III. 1698–1701. Maundy set. Rev. Numerals crowned. Fine to unc̄ir. 4 pieces

159 Anne. 1704–'13. Maundy set. Rev. 1, 2, 3, 4. crowned. Perfectly unc̄ir. or proof. 4 pieces

160 The same. 1711. Shilling; plain angles. Fair only

161 George I. 1723. Shilling. South Sea Co. variety. Very good; scarce.

162 The same. 1717–'27. Maundy set. Rev. 1, 2, 3, 4, crowned. Very fine; rare. 4 pieces

163 George II. 1741. Half crown, young head. Rev. Roses in angles. Very fine.

164 The same. 1758. Sixpence. Plain angles; very good.

165 The same. 1743–'46. Maundy set. Rev. 1, 2, 3, 4. crowned. Brilliant. 4 pieces

166 George III. 1787. Sixpence. Uncirculated.

167 The same. 1816. Shilling; bull head. Uncirculated.

168 The same. 1820. Half crown y stamped on the field. Very good.

169 The same. 1762–'86. Maundy set. Young head. Rev. Numerals crowned. Fine to proof. 4 pieces

170 The same. 1820. Maundy set. Old head. Proof. 4 pieces

171 The same. Shilling tokens. 1811 and '12. Birmingham Workhouse, Bristol, Fazeley, Gloucester, Mansfield, Poole, Stockport, Swansea, and one engraved. Good to fine; all scarce. 9 pieces

172 Fazeley. 1811. sixpence token; Bank of England. 1812, 1s. 6d. Fine. 2 pieces

173 George IV. 1821. Pistrucci crown. Barely fair.

174 The same. 1824 and 1825. Shilling and sixpence, by Pistrucci. Good and fine. 2 pieces

175 The same. 1825. Half crown and shilling, by Wyon. Good and fine. 2 pieces

176 The same. 1822–'27. Maundy set. Brilliant proofs. 4 ps

177 William IV. 1834–'36. 1½, 4, and 6 pence. Fine to uncirculated. 4 pieces

178 The same. 1836. Half crown and shilling. Unc. 2 pieces

179 The same. 1831. Maundy set by Wyon. Proof. 4 pieces

180 Victoria. 1846, '56, '59, '67. Half crowns; 3 Gothic. Good. 4 pieces

181 The same. 1838–'67. Shillings (9), sixpence (6), three pence (9), 2, and 1½ pence. Fair to uncir.; average very good. 21 pieces

182 1868-'73. Shilling, sixpence (2), Threepence. Uncirculated. 4 pieces

183 The same. 1866. Maundy money. 1, 2, 3, and 4 pence. Proof. 4 pieces

184 East India. Victoria. 1840. One rupee. Fine.

185 The same. 1862. Rupees. Slight varieties; very good and fine. 3 pieces

186 The same. 1840-'62. Half and quarter rupees, two annas. Good and fine. 5 pieces

187 English Colonial. One-eighth and one-sixteenth crown. Fine. 2 pieces

188 France. Early denarii, struck at Lyons. Very good. 2 pieces

189 William X, Duke of Aquitaine. Denarius. Very good.

190 Louis XIV. 1651. Halfcrown. Fine.

191 The same. 1703. Louis XV, 1728. 12 sous. Fine. 2 pcs

192 Louis XV. 1731. Isles du Vent. Very good; scarce. 13.

193 Louis XVI. 1786. Fourth crown. Fine.

194 The same. 1791. 30 sols. Rev. REGNE DE LA LOI. Varieties; very good. 2 pieces

195 Year 7. 5 francs. Hercules between Liberty and Justice; from different mints. Good. 2 pieces

196 Subalpine Gaul. 5 francs, year 10. Good.

197 Year 11. Bonaparte, " First consul." 5 francs. Good.

198 Napoleon I. 1810. 5 francs. Paris mint. Fine.

199 The same. 1811. 5 and 2 francs. Good. 2 pieces

200 The same. 1812. 5 francs. Very fine.

201 Charles X. 1825. 5 francs. A beautiful impression : sharp and uncirculated.

202 The same. 1825-'30. 2, 1, ½, and ¼ francs. Sharp and uncirculated. 4 pieces

203 The same. 1829. 5 francs. Fine.

204 Louis Philippe. 1836. 5 francs. Very fine.

205 The same. 1846. 50 centimes. Uncirculated.

206 The Republic. 1849. 5 francs. Hercules between two females. Uncirculated.

207 1850 5 francs. Head of Ceres. Fine.

208 Louis Napoleon. 1852. 5 francs. Uncirculated.

209 Napoleon III. 1855-'67. Francs ; different dates. Fine to uncirculated. 5 pieces

210 The same. 1866 and '67. 2 francs, 50 and 20 centimes. 4 pieces.

211 The same. 1868. 5 francs. Uncirculated.

212 The same. 1870. 5 francs. Uncirculated.

213 The Republic. 1870. 5 francs. Paris mint. Head of
Ceres. Rev. m.m. an anchor. Rare issue; uncir.

214 1871 and '72. 2 francs. Uncirculated. 2 pieces.

215 Guiana. (British) 1836. ½ and ¼ Guilder. Fine and
scarce. 2 pieces

216 Greece. Otho. 1855. Drachm. Fine.

217 Germany. Bavaria. Clemens Augustus. Mining half
crown. Bust in episcopal robes. Rev. Mining scene.
Fine; scarce. 22.

218 Maximilian Joseph. 1805. Crown. Bust and crowned
arms. Good.

219 Louis I. 1838 and '44. Half Gulden. Very good. 2 ps

220 Brunswick, Bremen, Hildesheim, Saxony, Anhalt, etc.
Early dates; good to fine. 9 to 14. 21 pieces

221 Brunswick. 1676 and 1706. XII and XXIV mariengroschen. Wild man with pine tree. Fine. 20 and
22. 2 pieces

222 1725-'86. II and VI mariengroschen. Wild man. Fine.
3 pieces

223 1621-1796. Bernberg. Fugger, Mecklenburg Schwerin
with Order of the Elephant around the shield, etc.
Average nearly half crown size. Fair only. 5 pieces

224 Glückstadt. 1644. III schil. Bust of Christian IV.
Very good. 12.

225 Hamburg. 1725-1855. 1 sechsling to 8 schilling. Several base; average very good. 9 to 19. 18 pieces

226 Lübeck. 1752. Crown of 48 schilling. Nearly fine.

227 Old denar. MONETA NOVA LVBE. Fine.

228 Maximilian (1610). Fourth crown as G. M. Order of
Teutonic Knights. Emperor in regalia. Rev. Knight
on horseback. Uncirculated; rare. 19.

229 Münster. 1659. View of the city and crowned arms.
Broad medallic crown. Good

230 Mecklenburg-Schwerin. 1825. Two-thirds thaler. Very
fine.

231 Nassau. Adolph. 1864. Vereinsthaler struck for 25th
anniversary of government. Uncirculated.

232 Prussia. Albert. 1535. Triplegross. Ornamental border
and loop soldered on coin. Fine. 16.

233 Frederic III. 1682. Two-thirds crown for Brandenburg.
Bust and arms. Fine.

234 1756, '71, and '72. One-sixth and one-third (2) thaler. Fair and good. 3 pieces

235 Frederic William III. 1799. 21 batz for Nenchatel and Vallon. Fair only ; rare. 22.

236 William and Augusta. Coronation thaler. Uncirculated

237 William. 1867. Vereinsthaler. Uncirculated.

238 Pfaltz. Alexander Sigismund. Archbishop. 1694. Crown : bust to right, and double shield crowned. Very good.

239 Saxony. John George. 1630. Centennial crown of Luther's confession at Augsburg, with bust of John, and date 1530, 25 *Junij* on reverse Very fine.

240 John George II. 1668. One-third crown, with bust. Fine.

241 John George III. 1684. Two-thirds crown : bust. Fine.

242 John George IV. 1693. Two-thirds crown : bust. Good.

243 1648, 1766. One-third and two-thirds (2) crown ; bust. Good and very good. 3 pieces

244 1690–1718. Obituary, religious jubilee, etc. Fair to fine. 12 to 17. 6 pieces

245 Anton, King, and Fred. August, co-regent. 1831. Crown commemorative of the re-organization of the State. Busts jugata and inscription. Very fine.

246 John V. 1867. Vereinsthaler. Very fine.

247 Saxe-Gotha. Frederic III. 1764. Two-thirds crown : bust. Fine

248 Saxe-Coburg Gotha. Ernest. 1869. Commemorative Vereinsthaler. Fine.

249 Schleswig-Holstein. Charles Frederic. 1711 and 1712. Fine. 13 2 pieces

250 Ulm. 1747. Cardinal Ferdinand inauguration medalet. Burning heart on altar, radiant triangle above. Rev. Inscription. Uncirculated. 17.

251 Wurtemburg and Nassau. 1838, and '64. Half gulden Very good. 3 pieces

252 Mining tokens. Hammers crossed and GLUCK AUF in wreath. Very fine and uncirculated. 12. 2 pieces

253 Minor coins of German States. 1734–1870. Chiefly base , average condition very fine. 55 pieces

254 Holland Gröningen groat, date MCCCCLXXVII. Very good ; one of the earliest coins with date. 16.

— 255 1568 Groningen great. Very good. 18
256 Zeeland. 1680. 30 stuber. Armed warrior behind shield and arms. Very good. 22.
257 1687 Crown. Armed warrior behind shield, and seven shields. Good.
258 1775 10 stubers. Liberty and crowned shield. Very fine. 17.
259 1686–1790. 1, 2, and 6 stubers of Deventer. W. Frisia, Zwolle, Zeeland, etc. Average good; several base.
12 pieces
260 William II. 1845 and '47. Gulden. Very good. 2 pieces
261 1848–'68. Half gulden, 25, 10, and 5 cents. Fine. 8 pcs
261a Dutch India. 1802–57. One-quarter (?), and one-tenth gulden. Good.
4 pieces
262 Hong Kong. VICTORIA QUEEN, 1866. Half dollar. Fine.
263 1867 Dollar.
264 1868 Dollar. Fine.
265 1865 and '66. 10 cents. Uncirculated.   2 pieces
266 1868 20 cents. Fine.
267 Hanover. George III. 1814. Two-thirds crown. Very fine; slightly scratched on reverse.
268 India. Thick old rupees. Native characters. Very good.
2 pieces
269 Rupees. Different types; native characters only. Fine.
3 pieces
270 Half rupees. Native characters; old and new types. Fine.
2 pieces
271 Rupee. 1749. Fine; very scarce.
272 Another. 1802. Fine.
273 Double (hamm) and another. Very fair. 8   2 pieces
274 Italy. Napoleon I. 1813. 5 francs; Milan mint. Very good.
275 Victor Emmanuel. 1850. One and one-half lire. Title "Re eletto." Florence mint. Very good. 3 pieces
276 The same. 1862. 2 and 1 lire. 50 and 20 centesimi. Fine. 4 pieces
277 The same. 1863 and '67. Lire (2), 50 (?), and 20 centesimi. Very good and fine. 7 pieces
278 The same. 1871. 5 lire. Very fine.
279 Humbert I. 1812. 5 lire. Uncirculated.
280 Lucca. Felix and Elisa. 1805. 1 franc; busts jugate, and value in wreath. Very fine and scarce.

281 Naples. Charles. 1749. Crown of 120 grani; title,
" Rex Neap. Hisp. Infans." River god reclining,
Vesuvius in the distance. Good : scarce.

282 1736 Half crown ; same type. Fair.

283 Bologna, Pisa, Ragusa. 20 soldi, etc. Fair to fine. 14
to 17.   3 pieces

284 Papal States. Benedict XIV. 1754. Crown by
Hamerani. Bust to right. Rev. Virgin with keys in
her right hand, and a temple in her left. Uncirculated ;
scarce.

285 Pius VI. 1780. Crown. Pontifical arms and Virgin
on clouds. Very fair.

286 Clement XI, Innocent XI and XII. Alex. VI, etc. Dime
to ¼ dollar size. One pierced. Very fine lot.   8 pcs

287 Gregory XVI, 1835 ; Pius IX, 1848. 20 baiocchi. Very
good and fine.   2 pieces

288 Pius IX. 1849. 5 baiocchi, *Rome* mint. Uncir. : scarce.

289 The same. 1850. 20 baiocchi. Uncirculated.

290 The same. 1861–'68. 5 baiocchi and 10 soldi. Fine. 4 ps

291 The same. 1866. 1 lira. Fine.   2 pieces

292 The same. 1868. 10 soldi. Fine.   3 pieces

293 Sardinia. Charles Felix. 1827. 2 lire. Very good.

294 Sicily. 1735–1798. Half and quarter crown, 20 and 5
grani. Average very fair.   9 pieces

294a Ferdinand IV. 1796. Crown of 120 grani. Good.

295 1818–'44. 5, 10, 20 grani, etc. Good to uncir. 5 pieces

296 Francis II. 1859. Crown of 120 grani. Fine.

297 Venice. Ludovico Manin. 1794. Crown. Female head
and Venetian lion. Good.

298 Ireland. Henry VIII. Groat : 3d coinage (1536–37).
English shield quartered by a cross and crowned. Rev.
Harp crowned. ~~Fine~~ and rare.

299 The same. Groat : 6th coinage (1541–3). Similar to last.
Fine : rare.

300 The same. Groat : 7th coinage (1544–5). Bust crowned,
nearly facing, and arms. CIVITAS DVBLINE : *m.m.* a
harp. Very fair ; scarce.

301 1805 and 1813. Bank tokens ; 10 pence Irish. Good
and very fine : scarce.   2 pieces

302 ~~Japan.~~ Bar of silver, quadrangular, impressed with
native characters on each side and counterstamped on
edge. Very fine and rare. 19 x 6.

303 Itzibu. Quadrangular. Uncirculated. 14 x 10.

304 Another.   Also uncirculated; scarce.

305 Fourth izzebue.   Very fine.   2 pieces

306 Dime size.   Recent coinage.   Uncirculated.

307 Luxemburg.   1790.   VI sols.   Uncirculated.   14

308 Malta.   Emmanuel Pinto.   1741.   2 taris.   Shield and
       Maltese cross.   Very good and scarce.   12.

309 Emmanuel de Rohan.   1777 and '79.   Taris: one poor,
       pierced, and base; the others very good. 10.   3 pieces

310 The same.   1796.   Crown.   Bust to right and shield.
       Good and scarce.

311 Mexico.   1742.   Half dollar; pillars crowned.   Very
       fair; scarce.

312 Charles IV, 1789 and '90; Augustine, 1822.   Proclama-
       tion medalets, average dime size; 2 pierced.   Very
       good and scarce.   4 pieces

313 Augustine.   1822.   Dollar.   Very good.

314 1824 Two reals or one-quarter dollar, "crook-neck."
       Very good.

315 1834 Dollar.   Good

316 1839 and '42.   Half dollars.   Fair.   2 pieces

317 1843 JURA DE LA CONSTITUCION MEXICANA.   Liberty
       seated.   Fine.   18.

318 1844 Dollar.   Very good.

319 1849 and '61.   Dollars.   Fine.   2 pieces

320 1863 Dollar.   Uncirculated.

321 Maximilian.   1864.   10 cents; Mexico mint.   Fine.

322 The same.   1864.   5 cents; same mint.   Very fine.

323 The same.   1864.   10 (3) and 5 cents.   Very good and
       fine.   5 pieces

324 The same.   1866.   Dollar: Mo mint.   Sharp and uncir.

325 The same.   1866.   Dollar: Mo. mint.   Very fine.

326 The same.   1866.   Dollar: Pi mint.   Legend in part
       weak, but fine.

327 The same.   1866.   Half dollar: Mo.   Fine.

328 The same.   1866.   Dime.   Mo. mint.   Very good.

329 1865 War medalet.   Beehive.   GRATITUD DEL PUEBL-
       ES 1865.   Rev. Trophy.   AL PRINCIPIO REAL DE DI-
       CIEMBRE.   Uncirculated; rare.   14.

330 Another.   Bust of Maximilian (?) to left.   14 stars below.
       Rev.   SALVA LA PATRIA DE LA ANARQUIA.   Fine;
       rare.   10.

331 Republic.   1887   Dollar.   Go. mint.   Uncirculated.

$\mathcal{S} \mathcal{S}^-$332 1868 Dollar.   Same mint.   Uncirculated.

$\mathcal{S} \mathcal{S}^-$333 1869 Dollar.   *Ca.* mint.   Uncirculated.

$\mathcal{S} \mathcal{S}^-$334 1870 Dollar.   *Pl.* mint.   Uncirculated.

$\rightarrow \mathcal{O}$ 335 1870 Half dollar.   Eagle and scales, surmounted by a
Liberty cap.   Fine.

$\mathcal{S} \mathcal{S}^-$ 336 1871 Dollar.   *Mo.* mint.   Same type as last.   Uncir.

337 1873 Dollar.   *Go.* mint.   Uncirculated.

338 1874 Dollars from diff. mints.   Fine and uncir.   2 pieces

/ $\mathcal{L}^-$ 339 1863–'74.   2 real or quarter dollar.   Different types or
dates: includes quarter dollar of Charles IV, reduced
to 20c. size and counterstamped with Chinese characters.   Very good and fine.   6 pieces

$\mathcal{L}$ 340 1822–1880.   Real of Augustine, pierced: 10 cents, inclusive of two of Maximilian (11), medios (3), and
cuartillos (4).   Very fine lot. .   . 19 pieces

$\mathcal{L} \mathcal{O}$ 341 Cob money.   Dollar.   Rude impression : pierced.

$\mathcal{I}$ 342 Cob money.   4 (1), 2 (3), and 1 (5) real.   One pierced.
Fair and good.   9 pieces

$\mathcal{2} \mathcal{S}^-$ 343 Newfoundland.   1872, 50 cents : 1865, 5 cents : also,
New Brunswick, 1862 and '64, 20 cents.   Average
fine.   4 pieces

/. / $\mathcal{S}^-$ 344 Poland.   Xaverius.   1756.   Crown : bust and arms.
Very good.

$\mathcal{S} \mathcal{S}^-$345 Stanislaus Augustus.   1794.   Crown of 6 zlot.   Legend
in part weak : about good.

/ $\mathcal{S}^-$ 346 1840 10 groszy.   Uncirculated.

// 347 Russia.   1757 and 1772.   5 and 10 kopees.   Fair and
good.   2 pieces

$\rightarrow \mathcal{S}^-$ 348 1813 and '17.   Rubel and half rubel.   Good and fair
2 pieces

$\rightarrow$ 349 1839 Three-quarter rubel, or 5 zlot.   Poor : scarce.

$\mathcal{L} \mathcal{S}^-$ 350 1840 Rubel.   Double-headed eagle, crowned, and inscription.   Good.

$\mathcal{L} \mathcal{S}^-$ 351 1844 Rubel.   Same type.   Very fine.

$\mathcal{L} \mathcal{S}^-$ 352 1854 Rubel.   Uncirculated.

353 1845–'71.   5, 10, 15, and 20 kopees.   Very good and fine.
6 pieces

/ $\mathcal{L}$ 354 1869 10, 15, and 20 kopees.   Uncirculated.   3 pieces

/ 3 355 1861–'66.   10, 15 kopees, 50 pennia, 1 mark.   All fine.
4 pieces

$\mathcal{L} \mathcal{C}$ 356 Siam.   Bullet money.   Half and quarter tical   Perfect;
rare.   3 pieces

$\mathcal{L}$ 357 One and half tical.   Perfect.   2 pieces

358 Scotland. Mary and Henry Darnley. 1565. Dollar. Arms of Scotland crowned, a thistle on each side in the field. Rev. Crowned palm tree. Barely fair, and remarkably small. Scarce.

359 James VI. 1602. Shilling or mark. Arms of Scotland crowned, and crowned thistle. Poor. 20.

360 Spain. Philip II. 1572. Bust to right. Great age; struck for Brabant. Good.

361 Charles III. 1712. Philip V. 1717. Louis, 1724. Philip V. 1725, 1738 (Chinese counterstamps). Charles III. 1783 and 1785, Charles IV, 1800. Ferdinand VII, 1811. 2 reales. Average good. 9 pieces

362 Charles III. 1775. Dollar. Numerous small counterstamps. Fair.

363 Gerona. 1808. Un duro, or necessity dollar. Counterstamped on each side. Good.

364 Joseph Napoleon. 1812. Dollar. Head rubbed; good and scarce.

365 Ferdinand VII, 1816, real, uncirculated; also Chas. IIII. 1798, real. Fine. 2 pieces

366 Isabella. 1864 and '68. 50 and 20 cents. Good and very fine. 2 pieces

367 1869 Provisional Government. 2 and 1 pesetas. Uncirculated. 2 pieces

368 Amadeus. 1871. 5 pesetas or francs. Uncirculated.

369 Charles II. 1685. 2 reales, crowned globe; do., 1684, 1690, 20 grani, crowned bust and golden fleece. Fair to very good; struck for Naples. 4 pieces

370 South America. Argentine Confederation. 1815, 2, 1820, 1, and 1849, 4 reales. Good. 5 pieces

371 Bolivia. 1835. Dollar. Bust of Bolivar and llamas under a tree. Fine.

372 1841-61. 4, 1, and half real. Good and fine. 8 pieces

373 1868 Melgarejo and Munez. Pacification medalets; two real size. Different; good and fine. 2 pieces

374 Colombia, 1821-64. 2, 1, and half real, counterstamped and pierced. Fair and good. 5 pieces

375 Costa Rica. 1850-65. Real 88 and 25 cents. Good. 4 pieces

376 Guatemala. Ferdinand VII. 1808, real; 1847, real (21 March). 2 pierced. Good. 3 pieces

377 1837 Metallic 2 reales. Radiant sun over altar. POR CONSTANCIA. Rev. Female crushing two snakes. EL PUEBLO ... Quarter dollar size; uncirculated.

378 New Granada. 1819. LIBERTAD AMERICANA. Struck over Caracas 2 real. Very good; scarce.

379 1840 8 reales. Eagle with scroll over cornucopia. Barely fair: scarce.

380 1838–'56. 2 (4), 1, and half real. Good to uncirculated
11 pieces

381 Cuartillas, or one-quarter real. Bogota mint. Fine.
3 pieces

382 Peru. 1827. Dollar. Liberty and shield. Abused and pierced.

383 1870 Dollar. Liberty seated, and shield. Fine.

384 1873 Dollar. Same type. Fine.

385 1850–'66. 2 (4), 1 (2), and half reales; also 1876, half real of Venezuela. Good to uncirculated. 8 pieces

386 Sweden. Charles XIV. 1821. Half species daler or 60 skilling, struck for Norway. Fine.

387 Oscar. 1856. One rigsdaler species. Bust and arms crowned, supported by two crowned lions. Very fine.

388 Charles XV. 1863. Four rigsdaler riksmark. Head to right and arms as before. Very fine or uncirculated.

389 1751 5 öre, 1845–'64, 10, 25 öre, etc. Good and fine; one base. 9 pieces

390 1827–'70. 2, 3, 12, and 24 (2) skilling for Norway. Good to uncirculated; two base. 6 pieces

391 Switzerland. 1851–'62. 2, 1, and half francs. Helvetia seated. Very good and fine. 4 pieces

392 Basle. Old Award medalet. Men cultivating and watering a vine. Rev. MAG BAS IVVENTVTI STVD. Fine. 18.

393 1810–'26. Aargau, Basle, and Berne. 5 batzen. Uncirculated. 3 pieces

394 Basle. 1810. 5 and 3 batzen. Uncir. 2 pieces

395 Berne. 1796. Half crown. Cantonal arms and Swiss warrior. Uncirculated.

396 Berne, Fribourg, Geneva, Lucerne, Soleure, 1710-1827, 1, 2½, 5 batzen, etc. Good to uncir. 6 pieces

397 Vaud. 1845. 1 franc. Uncirculated.

398 Zürich. 1794. Half crown. Arms and inscription. Uncirculated.

399 Cantonal batzen, 5, 10, 20, 25 centimes, etc. All base; average fine. 19 pieces

400 Turkey, etc. Abdul-Aziz. 10 piastres. Uncir. 24.

401 Mahmoud II. 5 piastres. In part weak; uncir. 22.

402 **Egypt.** Stars around Turkish and Arabic inscriptions. Uncirculated. 9 to 17. 4 pieces

403 Similar to last. Dime and quarter dollar size. Fine. 2 pieces

404 Quarter and half dollar size. Very good. 2 pieces

405 Miscellaneous. Turkish and Arabic inscriptions, etc. Good to uncirculated. 6 to 17. 7 pieces

GOLD COINS.

406 England. Anne. 1714. Sovereign. Bust to left and arms. Pierced over head. Good.

407 George II. 1752. Half sovereign. Good.

408 George III. 1803. Third guinea. Uncirculated.

409 France. Louis XVI. 1786. Louis d'or or 20 francs. Fine.

410 Holland. 1837. Ducat. Warrior with sword and fasces. Rev. Inscription. Uncirculated.

411 Hamburg. 1866. Ducat. Knight in armor with shield of city. Rev. Inscription. Nearly proof; rare.

412 Italy. Victor Emmanuel. 1863. 10 lire. Uncirculated.

413 Japan. Nibu. Thin oval coin, counterstamped on each side with Japanese characters. Very fine and rare. 22 x 13.

414 Fourth itzebue size. Base. 7 x 4.

415 United States. 1795. Half eagle. Close date, and lower curl between two points of star. Fine.

416 1795 Half eagle. Closer date; point of lower star barely touches curl. Fine.

417 1859 Dollar. Brilliant proof.

418 1860 Five dollars. Brilliant proof.

419 1860 Dollar. Brilliant proof.

420 1871 Dollar. Uncirculated.

421 1873 Dollar. Uncirculated.

422 Bechtler dollar. CAROLINA GOLD. 27 G. 21 c. Very fine.

423 Duplicate of last number. Same condition.

424 1852 Half dollar. CALIFORNIA GOLD. Fine.

425 1853 Dollar. CALIFORNIA GOLD. Varieties, both octagonal. Fine. 2 pieces

426 1853 Half dollar. CALIFORNIA GOLD. Varieties. Uncirculated. 2 pieces

427 1855 Quarter dollar. Octagonal: 1855, half (2) and
        quarter dollar; round and octagonal. Very fine. 4 ps

428 1854, '56, and '59. Quarter dollar. Octagonal. Fine :
        one pierced.   3 pieces

429 1855 Octagonal dollars. CALIFORNIA GOLD N. R. Un-
        circulated.   2 pieces

430 1864 Half and quarter dollar. Octagonal. The latter
        with ‡ in shield. Uncirculated.   2 pieces

431 1865 and '79. Half (2) and quarter dollar, one without
        date. Round and octagonal. Uncirculated. 6 pieces

432 1871 Half (4) and quarter dollar. Round and octagonal.
        Uncirculated.   7 pieces

433 1872. Half and quarter dollar. CALIFORNIA CHARM.
        Head of Washington. Uncirculated.   2 pieces

434 South America. Costa Rica. 1864. Dollar. Uncircu-
        lated.

435 Colombia. 1827. Dollar. Has been soldered on rev.
        for a button. Very good.

436 Turkey   Size of 20 franc piece. Fine.

UNITED STATES COINS.

PROOF SETS.

437 1856 Dollar, half dollar, quarter, dime, half dime, three
        cents, and nickel cent. *Fine proofs : rare.* 7 pieces

438 1858 *Fine proofs : very rare.*   7 pieces

439 1859 *Fine proofs : scarce.*   7 pieces

440 1860 *Fine proofs.*   7 pieces

441 1861 *Fine proofs.*   7 pieces

442 1862 *Fine proofs.*   7 pieces

443 1863 *Fine proofs.*   7 pieces

444 1864 Dollar, half dollar, quarter, dime, half dime, three
        cents, one cent nickel, two and one cent bronze. *Fine
        proofs.*   9 pieces

445 1865 Dollar, half, quarter, dime, half dime, three cents
        silver and nickel, two and one cent bronze. *Brilliant
        proofs.*   9 pieces

446 1866 Dollar, half, quarter, dime, half dime, three cents,
        five and three cents nickel, two and one cent bronze.
        Brilliant proofs.   10 pieces

447 1867 *Brilliant proofs.*   10 pieces

1868 *Brilliant proofs.* 10 pieces
1869 *Brilliant proofs.* 10 pieces
1870 *Brilliant proofs.* 10 pieces
1871 *Brilliant proofs.* 10 pieces
1872 *Brilliant proofs.* 10 pieces
1873 Old style. *Brilliant proofs.* 10 pieces
1873 Trade set. Dollar, half dollar, quarter, dime, five and three cents nickel, one cent bronze. *Brilliant proofs.* 7 pieces
1874 *Brilliant proofs.* 7 pieces
1875 *Brilliant proofs.* 7 pieces
1876 *Brilliant proofs.* 7 pieces
1877 Dollar, half dollar, quarter, twenty cents, dime, five and three cents nickel, one cent bronze. *Brilliant proofs.* 8 pieces
1878 Trade and standard dollars, half, quarter, twenty cents, dime, five and three cents nickel, one cent bronze. *Fine proofs.* 9 pieces
1879 Both dollars. *Brilliant proofs.* 8 pieces
1880 Both dollars. *Brilliant proofs.* 8 pieces
1881 Both dollars. *Brilliant proofs.* 8 pieces
MINOR PROOF SETS. 1864. Nickel cent, two and one cents bronze. *Brilliant proofs; rare.* 3 pieces
1865 3, 2, 1 cents. *Brilliant proofs.* 3 pieces
1866 5, 3, 2, 1 cents. *Brilliant proofs.* 4 pieces
1867 5, 3, 2 cents. *Brilliant proofs.* 3 pieces
1869 5, 3, 2, 1 cents. *Brilliant proofs.* 4 pieces
1870 5, 3, 2, 1 cents. *Brilliant proofs.* 4 pieces
1871 5, 3, 2, 1 cents. *Brilliant proofs.* 4 pieces
1872 5, 3, 2, 1 cents. *Brilliant proofs.* 4 pieces
1873 5, 3, 2, 1 cents. *Brilliant proofs; rare.* 4 pieces
1874 5, 3, 1 cents. *Brilliant proofs.* 3 pieces
1875 5, 3, 1 cents. *Brilliant proofs.* 3 pieces
1879 5, 3, 1 cents. *Brilliant proofs.* 3 pieces
1880 5, 3, 1 cents. *Brilliant proofs.* 3 pieces

DOLLARS.

1794 The date and stars to left; as usual, weak; the hair also rubbed from circulation. With these exceptions, and two trifling defects in the planchet, this dollar may be called good for this very rare date.

477 1795 Flowing hair. Lower curl far from lower star. Rev. 13 berries to wreath. Fine.

478 1795 Flowing hair. Lower curl touches point of star. Rev. 19 berries to wreath. Very good.

479 1795 Fillet head. Hair very little rubbed. Sharp and fine.

480 1796 Fillet head. 1 in date distant from lower curl. Rev. 8 berries to branch of laurel. Hair rubbed; fine.

481 1796 1 in date touches curl. Rev. 7 berries to branch of laurel. Rubbed; good.

482 1797 6 stars facing. Fine obverse; reverse good.

483 1797 7 stars facing. Fine.

484 1797 7 stars facing. Slightly larger date. Good.

485 1798 15 stars. Rev. Small eagle. Very good; rare.

486 1798 13 stars. Rev. Small eagle, Very good; rare.

487 1798 1 in date touches curl, and 8 the bust. Rev. Heraldic eagle. Barely circulated.

488 1798 Small date. Fine.

489 1798 Small date; die cracked through 9 of date, extending on each side below. Fine.

490 1798 Wide date, 8 touches the bust. Nearly fine.

491 1799 5 stars facing. Hair a little rubbed. Sharp and very fine. Rare.

492 1799 Lower star to right, distant from bust. Fine.

493 1799 Star slightly nearer bust. Very fine.

494 1799 Lower star still nearer bust. Nearly fine.

495 1800 Large date. Scratched in the field. Fine.

496 1800 Smaller date. 1 in date touches curl. Very good.

497 1801 Large date. Good.

498 1801 Smaller date. Hair a little rubbed. Sharp impression; fine.

499 1802 over '01. Hair rubbed. Fine.

500 1802 Fine.

501 1803 Very good.

502 1836 Goddess of Liberty seated; GOBRECHT at base; rev., Flying eagle: twenty-six stars in the field. Very fine; rare.

503 1840 Barely circulated.

504 1841 A few slight pin marks in the field; mint lustre. Uncirculated.

505 1842 Fine.

506 1843 Fine.

507 1844 Pin marks; very fine.
508 1845 Nearly fine.
509 1846 Fine.
510 1846 Orleans mint. Fine.
511 1847 Uncirculated.
512 1848 Uncirculated.
513 1849 Very fine.
514 1850 Very fine; scarce.
515 1852 Pierced above head. *Libbie*, engraved in the field. Good; very rare.
516 1853 Barely circulated; scarce.
517 1854 Extremely fine; rare.
518 1855 Nearly fine; rare.
519 1856 Fine. Very scarce.
520 1857 Fine. Scarce.
521 1859 Fine proof.
522 1859 Fine proof.
523 1859 Barely circulated.
524 1859 Orleans mint. Very good.
525 1860 Fine proof.
526 1860 Orleans mint. Pin marks in the field. Fine.
527 1861 Fine proof.
528 1862 Brilliant proof.
529 1863 Fine proof.
530 1864 Fine proof.
531 1865 Uncirculated.
532 1866 Brilliant proof.
533 1867 Fine proof.
534 1868 Brilliant proof.
535 1869 Brilliant proof.
536 1870 Fine proof.
537 1870 Fine.
538 1871 Brilliant proof.
539 1872 Brilliant proof.
540 1873 Old style. Brilliant proof.
541 1873 Trade dollar. Brilliant proof.
542 1873 Trade dollar. Brilliant proof.
543 1873 Another. Brilliant proof.
544 1874 Brilliant proof.
545 1875 Trade. Brilliant proof.

546 1876 Trade. Brilliant proof.
—547 1876 San Francisco. Uncirculated.
—548 1876 Carson City. Uncirculated.
549 1877 Trade. Brilliant proof.
550 1877 San Francisco. Uncirculated.
—551 1877 Carson City. Uncirculated.
552 1878 Trade. Brilliant proof.
553 1878 San Francisco. Uncirculated.
554 1878 Standard. Fine proof.
555 1878 Standard. Uncirculated.
556 1878 Standard. San Francisco mint. Uncirculated.
—557 1881 Trade. Brilliant proof.

HALF DOLLARS.

558 1794 Lower star on right touches bust, on left pierces curl. Date, legend and stars all very good. Nearly fine ; rare.

559 1795 Lower curl pressed between two points of star, curving upward ; second curl touches second star. Rare variety ; extremely fine.

560 1795 Lower curl between and over two points of star, without touching ; nearly fine.

561 1795 Lower curl between and over lower stars. Fine.

562 1795 Lower star pierces lower curl. Very good.

563 1795 Two lower curls point to two lower stars. Good.

564 1796 Fifteen stars. Prominent parts rubbed, but everything very plain. Strictly good ; very rare.

565 1796 Sixteen stars. Hair and eagle's breast rubbed ; the legends and date strong, the stars broad and well struck. Fine ; very rare.

566 1797 The hair and eagle's breast a trifle rubbed, stars on the right a little flattened ; with these exceptions this piece is in strictly fine condition. One of the best half dollars of this date I have seen : very rare.

567 1801 Very good ; rare.

568 1802 Very fine ; rare.

569 1803 Very fine ; scarce.

570 1804 under '05. Fine ; scarce.

571 1805 Very good.

572 1806 Blunt 6. Very fine.

573 1806 Pointed 6. Cracked die ; fine.

574 1806 Pointed 6. Fine.

575 1807 Head to right. Fine.

576 1807 Duplicates. Very good.   2 pieces

577 1807 Head to left. Fine.

578 1807 Another. Very good.

579 1808 over '07. Fine; scarce.

580 1808 Very fair.   2 pieces

581 1809 Fine.

582 1809 Another. Good.

583 1810 Fine.

584 1810 Another. Good.

585 18⬤11 Uncirculated; scarce.

586 1811 Very good.

587 1811 Duplicates. Good.   2 pieces

588 1812 Uncirculated.

589 1812 Another. Uncirculated.

590 1812 Fine.   2 pieces

591 1813 Uncirculated.

592 1813 Very good.   2 pieces

593 1814 over '13. Very fine; rare.

594 1814 Very fine.

595 1814 From different dies. Very fine.   2 pieces

596 1815 Fine, but scratched in the field before bust. Rare.

597 1817 over '13. Sharp; uncirculated.

598 1817 over '13. Fine.

599 1817 Perfect die. Uncirculated.

600 1817 Another. Very fine.

601 1818 over '17. Uncirculated.

602 1818 over '17. From different dies; the stars on each side much nearer the head. Extremely fine.

603 1818 Perfect die. Fine.

604 1819 Uncirculated.

605 1819 From different dies. Very fine.   2 pieces

606 1820 over '19. Very good.

607 1820 Wide date; fine.

608 1821 Uncirculated.

609 1821 Close date; fine.

610 1822 Very fine.

611 1823 Uncirculated.

612 1823 From different dies. Very good.   2 pieces

613　1824 over previons date or dates. It was at one time asserted that the last figure in the date of this variety had been recut two or three times ; to judge from the appearance of this specimen, a perfect, sharp impression, nothing positive can be asserted, though the outer curve under the 4 bears a strong resemblance to a 2 or 3. Uncirculated ; very scarce.

614　1824 From different dies. Very fine and uncir.　2 pcs

615　1824 Very close date : 4 in date almost grazes 2. Very good.

616　1825 Uncirculated.

617　1825 From different dies. Very fine.　2 pieces

618　1826 Uncirculated.

619　1826 From different dies. Uncirculated.　2 pieces

620　1826 From different dies. Nearly fine.　2 pieces

621　1827 Large date. Very fine.

622　1827 Small date. Uncirculated.

623　1827 All the stars and the 7 in date extend to border, good ; another, small date, fine.　2 pieces

624　1828 Sharp and uncirculated. A beautiful half dollar

625　1828 Very fine.

626　1829 Sharp and uncirculated ; a splendid impression.

627　1829 Uncirculated.

628　1829 Fine.　2 pieces

629　1830 Uncirculated.

630　1830 Large and small 0 in date. Very fine.　2 pieces

631　1831 Uncirculated.

632　1831 From different dies. Fine.　2 pieces

633　1832 Uncirculated.

634　1832 From different dies. Fine.　2 pieces

635　1833 Uncirculated.

636　1833 Fine.　2 pieces

637　1834 Large date ; large lettering on rev. Uncirculated.

638　1834 Large date ; small lettering on rev. Uncirculated.

639　1834 Large date : large blurred 4 : small lettering on rev. Fine.

640　1834 Small date. Uncirculated.

641　1834 Small date. From different rev. dies. Fine.　2 ps

642　1835 Very fine.

643　1836 Uncirculated.

644　1836 From different dies. Uncirculated.　2 pieces

645 1836 Reeded edge. Very fine.

646 1837 Extremely fine.

647 1837 Same condition.

648 1838 Uncirculated.

649 1838 Extremely fine.

650 1839 Uncirculated; scarce.

651 1839 Very fine.

652 1839 O. for Orleans under the bust. Fine; scarce.

653 1839 Liberty seated. Fine.

654 1840 Uncirculated; mint lustre.

655 1840 Orleans. Very good.

656 1841 Orleans. Very fine.

657 1842 Large date. Fine.

658 1842 Small date. Very fine.

659 1842 Orleans. Fine.

660 1843 Fine.

661 1843 Orleans mint. Fine.

662 1844 Fine.

663 1844 Orleans mint. Fine.

664 **1845 Fine.**

665 1845 Orleans mint. Fine.

666 1846 Uncirculated.

667 1846 6 in date doubly struck. Extremely fine.

668 1846 Orleans mint. Very good.

669 1847 Uncirculated.

670 1847 Orleans mint. Fine.

671 1848 Uncirculated.

672 1848 Orleans mint. Fine.

673 1849 Fine.

674 1850 Mint lustre; sharp and uncirculated.

675 1850 Orleans mint. Fine.

676 1851 Very fine; scarce.

677 1851 Orleans mint. Very good; scarce.

678 1852 Uncirculated.

679 1853 Orleans mint. Fine.

680 1854 Fine.

681 1854 Orleans mint. From different dies. Both very fine.
2 pieces

682 1855 Fine.

683 1855 Orleans mint. Uncirculated.

684 1856 Orleans mint. Extremely fine.
685 1857 Uncirculated.
686 1857 Orleans mint. Fine.
687 1858 Uncirculated.
688 1858 Orleans mint. Fine.
689 1856 and '58. San Francisco mint. Poor and good.
2 pieces
690 1859 Fine proof.
691 1859 Uncirculated.
692 1859 Orleans and San Francisco mints. Good. 2 pieces
693 1860 Fine proof.
694 1860 Philadelphia and Orleans mints. Very fine. 2 pieces
695 1861 Uncirculated.
696 1861 Uncirculated.
697 1861 Orleans. Fine.
698 1861 Orleans and San Francisco mints. Fine. 2 pcs.
699 1862 Fine proof.
700 1862 San Francisco. Fine.
701 1863 Proof.
702 1863 San Francisco. Fine.
703 1864 Proof.
704 1864 San Francisco mint. Good.
705 1865 Fine proof.
706 1865 San Francisco mint. Good; scratched.
707 1866 Fine proof
708 1866 San Francisco mint. With and without motto on
rev. Good. 2 pieces
709 1867 Brilliant proof.
710 1867 San Francisco mint. Nearly fine.
711 1868 Fine proof.
712 1868 San Francisco mint. Nearly fine.
713 1869 Fine proof.
714 1869 Uncirculated.
715 1869 San Francisco mint. Very good.
716 1870 Brilliant proof.
717 1870 Uncirculated
718 1871 Philadelphia and San Francisco mints. Uncirculated. 2 pieces
719 1872 Fine proof.
720 1872 San Francisco mint. Fine.

1873 Arrows. Fine proof.

1873 Without arrows. Brilliant proof.

1873 Carson City mint. Fine.

1874 Brilliant proof.

1874 Carson City. Fine.

1875 Brilliant proof.

1875 San Francisco and Carson City. Uncirculated.
2 pieces

1876 Tarnished proof.

1876 San Francisco. Uncirculated.

1876 Carson City. Uncirculated.

1876 San Francisco and Carson City. Uncirculated. 2 ps

1877 Uncirculated.

1877 San Francisco mint. Uncirculated.

1877 San Francisco mint. Uncirculated. 2 pieces

1877 Carson City mint. Very fine.

1878 Fine.

QUARTER DOLLARS.

1796 Much worn, obv. and rev., the date plain. Barely
fair but scarce.

1804 Sharp, perfect impression. Barely circulated, and
one of the few strictly fine quarter dollars of this date
known. Very rare.

1804 Good ; scarce.

1805 Fine ; scarce.

1806 over '05. Very fair.

1806 Pointed 6. Fine ; nicked.

1806 Pointed 6. Fine.

1807 Very fair.

1815 Very good.

1805, '06, '07 and '15. Good. 4 pieces

1818 Very fine.

1819 Fine.

1820 Good.

1821 Mint lustre ; sharp and uncirculated. Rare in this
condition.

1822 Fair.

1824 Nearly fine.

1825 Nearly fine.

1828 Fine.

755 1818–'28 Fair to good.   7 pieces
756 1831 Uncirculated.
757 1831 Uncirculated.   2 pieces
758 1832, '33, '34, and '35.   Fine.   4 pieces
759 1836 Uncirculated.
760 1836, '37, and '38 both types.   Good.   4 pieces
761 1837 Uncirculated.
762 1838 Head of Liberty, and Liberty seated. V. fine.   2 ps
763 1839 Very fine.
764 1840 Very fine.
765 1841 Uncirculated.
766 1842 Fine.
767 1840, '41, '42, '43, and '44.   Orleans mint.   Very good
      and fine.   5 pieces
768 1845 Barely circulated.
769 1846 Uncirculated.
770 1847 Very fine.
771 1847 Orleans mint.   Uncirculated.
772 1849 ~~Uncirculated~~.
773 1850 Phila. and Orleans.   Very fine.   2 pieces
774 1851 Phila. and Orleans.   Very good.   2 pieces
775 1847, '48, '50, '51, and '52.   Very good.   5 pieces
776 1853 *Without arrows.*   Uncirculated ; very rare.
777 1853 Arrows.   Philadelphia and Orleans.   Very good or
      fine.   2 pieces
778 1854 Phila. and Orleans.   Fine.   2 pieces
779 1855 Uncirculated.
780 1855 and '56.   San Francisco.   Fair : very scarce.   2 ps
781 1856 Phila. and Orleans.   Uncirculated.   2 pieces
782 1857 Phila. and Orleans.   Very fine.   2 pieces
783 1858 Uncirculated.
784 1858 Phila. and Orleans.   Fine and good.   2 pieces
785 1859 Proof.
786 1859 Uncirculated.
787 1860 Fine proof.
788 1860 Orleans.   Very fine.
789 1861 Fine proof.
790 1861 Uncirculated.   2 pieces
791 1862 Fine proof.
792 1862 Uncirculated.   2 pieces

793 1863 Fine proof.
794 1863 Uncirculated.
795 1864 Proof.
796 1864 Uncirculated.
797 1865 Fine proof.
798 1865 and '66 San Francisco. Fine.   2 pieces
799 1866 Brilliant proof.
800 1867 Brilliant proof.
801 1868 Brilliant proof.
802 1869 Brilliant proof.
803 1869 Brilliant proof.
804 1869 San Francisco. Fine.
805 1870 Brilliant proof.
806 1871 Brilliant proof.
807 1872 Brilliant proof.
808 1872 San Francisco. Very fine.
809 1873 Without arrows. Brilliant proof.
810 1873 Arrows. Brilliant proof.
811 1873 Phila. and San Francisco mints. Uncirc. 2 pieces
812 1874 Brilliant proof.
813 1874 S., 1875 S. & C.C., 1876, S. & C.C. Fine to uncirculated.   5 pieces
814 1875 Brilliant proof.
815 1876 Uncirculated.
816 1876 Uncirculated.   2 pieces
817 1877 Uncirculated.
818 1877 Duplicates. Uncir.   2 pieces
819 1877 San Frisco and Carson City mints. Uncir. 2 pieces
820 1878 Fine proof.
821 1879 Brilliant proof.
822 1880 Brilliant proof.
823 TWENTY CENTS. 1875. Proof.

DIMES.

824 1796 Perfect die. 6 in date distant from bust. Very fine; rare.
825 1796 The 6 in date touches bust; coarse break in the from star to border. Fine; rare.
826 1796 Duplicate of last number. Very fair.
827 1796 The 6 in date touches bust. Break in the die from 1 to 9 through the date. Nearly fine.

828 1796 Duplicate of last number. Fair.

829 1797 Sixteen stars. Very good : rare.

830 1797 Thirteen stars. The hair rubbed, otherwise equal to last. Rare.

831 1798 over '97. Very good ; pin scratch on obverse. Rare.

832 1798 Perfect date. Date and legend plain. Barely fair obverse, the rev. better.

833 1800 Hair rubbed smooth. Very fair.

834 1801 Date plain. Poor.

835 1802 Date, legend, and stars very good, the hair worn smooth. Rev. Better than obverse. Except one, rarest date of the dimes.

836 1803 Same condition as last. Rare.

837 1804 Legend, date, and stars, except on the left, very good, the hair shows all the heavier lines. Rev. Good, a little weak near edge. The rarest date of dimes.

838 1805 A very fine dime ; barely if at all circulated.

839 1805 Very good.

840 1805 Good.   2 pieces

841 1807 Some stars on left and part of legend on rev. nearest edge feebly struck. Extremely fine dime. Very scarce.

842 1807 Very fair.

843 1809 Good ; scarce.

844 1811 Very good ; scarce.

845 1814 Fine. Scarce.

846 1820 Large and small dates. Fine.   2 pieces

847 1821 Small date. Very fine.

848 1821 Medium date. Nearly fine.

849 1821 Large date. Fine.

850 1822 Poor : date legible. Rare.

851 1822 A trifle better than last; date legible. Rare.

852 1823 over '22. Very good.

853 1824 over '23. Very fine.

854 1827 Large date. Uncirculated.

855 1828 Uncirculated.

856 1829 Uncirculated.

857 1831 Mint lustre. Uncirculated.

858 1832 Uncirculated.

859 1833 Uncirculated.

860 1834 Large and small dates. Very fine and uncir. 2 pieces

861 1835 and '36. Fine.   2 pieces

862 1836 Uncirculated.
863 1837 From different dies. Uncirculated. 2 pieces
864 1837 Liberty seated, without stars. Fine proof.
865 1838 Liberty seated, without stars. O. mint. Very good.
866 1838 Liberty seated; stars. Uncirculated.
867 1840 Without drapery under the elbow. Uncirculated.
868 1841 Drapery under the elbow. Uncirculated.
869 1843 Uncirculated.
870 1845 Orleans mint. Very fine.
871 1846 Very good; scarce.
872 1846 Very good; scarce.
873 1852 Orleans. Uncirculated.
874 1853 Without arrows. Fine.
875 1853 Arrows. Uncirculated.
876 1853 With and without arrows. Uncir. 2 pieces
877 1854, '55 and '56. Uncir. 3 pieces
878 1857 Orleans. Brilliant; uncirculated.
879 1858 Uncirculated.
880 1859 Fine proof.
881 1859 Orleans. Uncir.
882 1860 Stars. San Francisco mint. Uncir.; scarce.
883 1860 Without stars. Fine proof.
884 1861 Fine proof.
885 1862 Fine proof.
886 1863 Brilliant proof.
887 1864 Fine proof.
888 1865 Brilliant proof.
889 1867 Brilliant proof.
890 1868 Brilliant proof.
891 1869 Brilliant proof.
892 1861, '62, '65, '67, '68, '69 and '70. Uncirculated. 7 pieces
893 1870 Brilliant proof.
894 1871 Brilliant proof.
895 1872 Brilliant proof.
896 1873 Without arrows. Brilliant proof.
897 1873 Arrows. Brilliant proof.
898 1874 Brilliant proof.
899 1875 Brilliant proof.
900 1876 Phila., San Fran., Carson City. Uncir. 3 pieces
901 1877 San Francisco and Carson City. Uncir. 3 pieces
902 1873, '74, '75, '78 and '82. Uncirculated. 5 pieces

HALF DIMES.

903 1794 Considerably circulated but good ; rare.

904 1794 Stars to right very weak.   About equal to last.

905 1795 Lower stars touch the point of bust and second hair-lock. Fine.

906 1795 Star does not touch point of bust : coarse second hair-lock between points of lower star   Very good.

907 1796 ~~Strictly~~ fine ; rare.

908 1797 Thirteen stars. Good ; rare.

909 1797 Fifteen stars.   A little better than the last ; small nicks in the centre. Rare.

910 1797 Sixteen stars. Fine, but a letter engraved on each side. Rare.

911 1800 Fine ; scarce.

912 1800 Another. Very good.

913 1801 Very good, but nicked in the field. Rare.

914 1803 Good : pierced through legend. Rare.

915 1805 Small nicks, obv. and rev., and hair rubbed. Date, legend, stars all very good. Rare. •

916 1829 Mint lustre. Uncirculated.

917 1829 Uncirculated.

918 1830 Perfect date, and 0 in date very high. Unc. 2 pcs

919 1831 Uncirculated.

920 1832, '34, '35, and '37. Uncirculated.   4 pieces

921 1837 Liberty seated, without stars. Mint lustre : uncir.

922 1838 Liberty seated : stars. Uncirculated.

923 1839 Uncirculated.

924 1840 Liberty seated, without drapery under the elbow. Uncirculated.

925 1840 Liberty seated, with drapery. Uncirculated.

926 1841 Drapery. Perfectly uncirculated.

927 1842 Drapery. Perfectly uncirculated.

928 1843 Perfectly uncirculated.

929 1844 Perfectly uncirculated.

930 1845 Uncirculated.

931 1846 Good ; rare.

932 1849–'52 inclusive. Uncirculated.   4 pieces

933 1853 With and without arrows. Uncir.   2 pieces

934 1854 and '55. Uncirculated.   2 pieces

935 1856, '57, and '58. Uncirculated.   3 pieces

936 1860 Proof.
937 1860 Orleans. o, under the wreath. Fine.
938 1861 Proof.
939 1862 Fine proof.
940 1862 Uncirculated.   2 pieces
941 1864 Fine proof.
942 1865 Fine proof.
943 1866 Brilliant proof.
944 1867 Brilliant proof.
945 1868 Brilliant proof.
946 1869 Brilliant proof.
947 1870 Brilliant proof.
948 1870 Brilliant proof.
949 1871 Brilliant proof.
950 1872 Brilliant proof.
951 1873 Brilliant proof.

THREE CENTS.

952 1851 Orleans. Uncirculated.   2 pieces
953 1851 Orleans. Uncir.   6 pieces
954 1853–'61 inclusive. Average, very good.   8 pieces
955 1861 Large date. Fine.
956 1862 Perfectly uncirculated.   2 pieces
957 1862 Perfectly uncirc. Good lot for a dealer.   8 pieces
958 1862 Proof.
959 1868 Proof.
960 1869 Brilliant proof.
961 1871 Brilliant proof.
962 1872 Brilliant proof.
963 1873 Brilliant proof.

UNITED STATES CENTS.

With reference to "Monograph of United States Coins and their Cents," by Ed. Frossard.

964 1793 Head of Liberty. Rev. Chain of thirteen links. UNITED STATES OF AMERI. Rarely fair; scratched.
965 1793 Head of Liberty, a sprig of laurel under the bust. Rev. ONE CENT in wreath, vine and bars on edge. A perfect and very strong impression, of beautiful light brown color, and entirely uncirculated. Excessively rare and desirable. Monng. No. 7, 2nd rev.

38   *United States Cents.*

966 1793 Wreath. Very good. Monog. No. 7, 2d rev.
967 1793 Wreath. Good. Monog. No. 7. 1st rev.
968 1793 Wreath. Beautifully tooled, obverse and reverse. Extremely fine and deceiving.
969 1793 Liberty cap. Fair: very scarce.
970 1794 *The Ornate.* Hair flattened. A fine and scarce cent. Monog. 11; Maris 25.
971 1794 *Fallen* 4. Deep, even milling, a perfect impression, slightly bruised on edge. Very fine. Monograph 12: Maris 20.
972 1794 *Short bust.* Fine. Monog. 13: Maris 22.
973 1794 *Patagonian.* Fine. Monog. 14: Maris 24.
974 1794 *Amiable face.* Hair slightly flattened, and rev. in part weak. but fine. Monog. 16: Maris 26.
975 1794 *Shielded hair.* Crack in die between E and S of STATES on rev. Olive color; a fine cent. Monog. 19: Maris 32.
976 1794 *Sans milling.* Fine: light milling on nearly entire circumference. Monog. 22: Maris 3.
977 1794 *Plicae.* Well struck: nearly fine. Monog. 20: Maris 37.
978 1794 *Plicae.* A variety; break in die between T and Y in LIBERTY. Very good: small cut in the field.
979 1794 Varieties. Good. 2 pieces
980 1794 Varieties. Fair. 2 pieces
981 1795 Thick pl., lettered edge. Very fair and scarce.
982 1795 Thin pl. Rev. ONE CENT high. Very good.
983 1795 Thin pl Rev. ONE CENT in centre. Good.
984 1796 Liberty cap. 6 in date distant from bust. Nearly fine but spotted obverse. with a fine reverse. Very scarce.
985 1796 Liberty cap. The 6 in date nearer the bust: L in LIBERTY touches cap. Good: scarce.
986 1796 Liberty cap. The 1 in date touches hair, and 6 close to bust. Good: scarce.
987 1796 Fillet head. The 6 in date touches bust. Planchet a little rough on both sides. A beautiful cent. of fine color, barely if at all circulated.' Very rare.
988 1796 Fillet head. The 6 in date distant from bust. Nearly fine.
989 1797 Original dull red color. Uncirculated: rare.
990 1798 Wide date. Very good.
991 1798 Closer date. Olive color. fine.

992 1798 Another. Fine.

993 1799 The '99 knobbed, and slanting. Unusually fine, the date, legend, and head equally perfect. Small scratch to left on hair-locks. Of uniform brown color, fine and very rare.

994 1799 The date unusually well struck, legend and date very good. The rev. shows break under a of one distinctly. For the most authentic variety of 1799 cents, fine; in fact, one of the best I have seen, though in condition not quite equal to last. Very rare and desirable.

995 1800 over '99. Dark; ...

996 1800 Perfect date. Olive color; a little weak through legend on obv., but uncirculated. Rare.

997 1801 Rev. ... and ... Good. 2 pieces.

998 1802 Very fine obverse of reddish color. Reverse fine. scarce.

999 1802 Dark olive; fine.

1000 1802 From different dies. Very good. 2 pieces.

1001 1803 Very fine impression, but scratched through face on obverse.

1002 1803 Another. The hair a little worn, but a strictly fine cent.

1003 1803 Rev. ... over ... Rare variety; good.

1004 1804 Perfect die. Very fair or good for date. Rare.

1005 1804 Broken die. Good; small scratch on head.

1006 1805 Olive color. A very beautiful cent; perfect impression and uncirculated. Rare. ...

1007 1805 Extremely fine; in some respects equal to last.

1008 1805 Extremely fine; pin nick in the field. Rare.

1009 1806 Fine; very good color. Rare. ...

1010 1807 over '06. Very good indeed.

1011 1807 Perfect date. Rev. Edge bruised; fine.

1012 1808 So-called twelve star variety. Good and scarce.

1013 1808 Thirteen stars. Good; ...

1014 1809 Bronze color. Fine light impression; ... A beautiful and rare coin.

1015 1810 Companion piece to last quarter, in precisely the same condition. Rare. ...

1016 1810 Very good.

1017 1811 over '10. Good and scarce.

1018 1811 Perfect date. Slightly ... nearly fine.

1019 1812 Fine.

1020 1812 Slightly misstruck. A trifle finer than last.

1021 1813 Fine : dark. Very scarce.

1022 1814 Plain 4. Fine and scarce.

1023 1814 Bearded chin. Plain 4, and small break in die on the chin. whence this variety derives its name. Very fine ; scarce.

1024 1814 Crossed 4. Rough surface ; very fine.

1025 1815 Bogus.

1026 1816 Perfect die. Dark : very fine.

1027 1816 Break in die on edge. Olive color ; uncir.

1028 1 8 17 Bright red ; uncirculated.

1029 Varieties. Brown color, and olive. Very fine. 2 pieces

1030 1817 15 stars. Dark ; fine.

1031 1818 Connected stars. Nearly bright red ; uncirc.

1032 1819 Small date. Cracked die ; bright red, and nearly proof surface.

1033 1819 From different dies. All very fine.   4 pieces

1034 1820 Perfect die. Red and uncirculated.

1035 1820 Connected stars. Bright red and a beautiful cent.

1036 1820 Varieties, one with 1 in date far from 8. Fine. 2 pieces

1037 1821 Strong impression. Very fine ; rare.

1038 1822 Fine ; small scratch over head.

1039 1823 A few stars slightly rounded, but a sharp beautiful impression. Olive color. barely if at all circulated. Very rare.

1040 1823 Mint restrike. from the cracked die. Bright red.

1041 1824 Dark. Fine and scarce.

1042 1825 All the stars broad and flat. An extremely fine impression ; uncirculated.

1043 1826 Fine impression and color.

1044 1827 Dark ; fine.

1045 1828 Very good. *clean and red*

1046 1829 Very good.

1047 1830 Olive color. Uncirculated, but scratched through one star.

1048 1830 The peculiarity of this cent is a light break in the die, having the appearance of a circle. which follows the entire circumference, near the milling. Fine.

1049 1831 Very good.

1050 1832 Olive color. Very fine and rare.

1051 1833 Very fine.

1052 1834 Very fine.

1053 1835 Olive color. Very fine.

1054 1836 Perfect die. Very fine.

1055 1836 Break in die on edge. Fine.

1056 1837 Plain hair-string, stars weak. Bright red.

1057 1837 Plain hairstring, light impression. Very fine.

1058 1837 Beaded hairstring. A few stars touched : hardly if at all circulated. Very scarce.

1059 1838 Thin planchet, size 17. Good.

1060 1838 Beaded hair-string. Extremely fine.

1061 1839 '40 head. Very fine : dark purple.

1062 1840 Straight date. Red and uncirculated.

1063 1840 Curved date. Uncirculated.

1064 1841 Fine.

1065 1842 Large date. Uncirculated. A very beautiful cent, nearly proof obverse.

1066 1842 Small date. Dark : barely circulated.

1067 1843 The three varieties. Very fine and scarce. 3 pcs.

1068 1844 Uncirculated.

1069 1845 Very fine.

1070 1846 Uncirculated.

1071 1847 Uncirculated.

1072 1848 Very fine.

1073 1849 Light bronze color. Uncirculated.

1074 1850 Bright red.

1075 1851 Bright red.

1076 1852 Bright red.

1077 1853 Uncirculated.

1078 1854 Dull red. Uncirculated.

1079 1855 Bright red. Uncirculated.

1080 1855 Dull red. Uncirculated.

1081 1856 Bright red. Uncirculated.

1082 1856 Duplicates. Uncirculated.   3 pieces

1083 1857 Large date. Uncirculated.

1084 1857 Small date. Fine proof ; very scarce.

1085 1857 Small date. Uncirculated.

1086 1793–1857 Set of cents. Includes all dates and several
varieties of dates, as Liberty cap and fillet head of
1796—excepting 1799, 1804, and 1809. Average condition very fair or good, and a desirable set either for
a dealer or beginner. 68 pieces

1087 1794–1857. Includes a very large number of early dates.
Poor to fine ; average condition very fair, a few only
pierced. 790 pieces

I will state for the benefit of buyers that I have very frequently seen
cents not a whit better than very many in the last lot catalogued singly
and bring more than enough to warrant the extra expenditure in the
printing

HALF CENTS.

1088 1793 Good. Monog. obv. 1 with rev. of No. 2. Unpublished combination.

1089 1793 Nearly fine, good color. Monog. No. 4.

1090 1794 Fine ; scarce. Monog. No. 2.

1091 1794 Slight scratch on obv.: break in die on reverse.
Very fine ; scarce. Monog. No. 3.

1092 1794 Perfect die. Good. Monog. No. 3.

1093 1794 Nicked on obv. Good. Monog. No. 4.

1094 1795 Lettered edge. Very good and scarce.

1095 1795 Thin planchet. From different dies: good and
scarce.

1096 1796 *Edwards dies.* Sharp: bright red. Only a few
specimens struck, the dies destroyed. Rare.

1097 1797 Crack in die from hair to 1 of date. Good.

1098 1797 From different dies. Very fair. 2 pieces

1099 1800 Fine.

1100 1802 Very fair: every thing distinct.

1101 1802 Another. Only fair

1102 1803 Olive color. A few leaves on rev. weak. Uncir.

1103 1804 Stemless wreath. Very fine.

1104 1805 Stemless wreath. Very fine : scarce.

1105 1806 Bright red. Uncirculated.

1106 1807 and '08. Good. 2 pieces

1107 1809 Olive color. Very fine.

1108 1810 Good : scarce.

1109 1811 Good : very scarce.

1110 1825 and '26. Very fine. 2 pieces

1828 13 stars. Brilliant light bronze color. Sharp and
    uncirculated.

1828 12 and 13 stars. Fine and unc'ir.   2 pieces

1829 Very fine.

1831 Altered date. Good.

1832 to '35 inclusive. Uncirculated.   4 pieces

1836 Reddish purple. Original. *Fine proof ; rare.*

1837 " Half cent worth." Very fine; scarce.

1840 Mint restrike. *Fine proof. rare.*

1841 Mint restrike. *Fine proof ; rare.*

1842 Weak impression, mint restrike. *Proof ; rare.*

1843 Mint restrike. *Fine proof. rare.*

1844 Mint restrike. *Fine proof ; rare.*

1845 Mint restrike. *Fine proof ; rare.*

1846 Mint restrike. *Fine proof ; rare.*

1847 Mint restrike. *Fine proof ; rare.*

1848 Mint restrike. *Fine proof ; rare.*

1849 Small date. Original. *Fine proof ; rare.*

1849, large date, and 1850. Good and fine.   2 pieces

1851 Uncirculated.

1852 Original. *Dull proof ; rare.*

1853 and '54. Uncirculated.   2 pieces

1855 *Brilliant proof ;* very scarce.

1856 Uncirculated.

1857 Uncirculated.

1795 Fine electrotype: 1794, '97, 1802 to 1809, and
    various dates to 1857. Average good, several very
    scarce.   32 pieces

MISCELLANEOUS.

NICKEL CENTS. 1856. Very fine; scarce.

1857-'61. Fine to uncirculated.   8 pieces

1857 Flying phallus, etc. Tinted.   2 pieces

BRONZE CENTS. 1864-1883, lacking 1877 only. Bright
    red ; uncirculated.   19 pieces

TWO CENTS. BRONZE. 1864 to 1872, inclusive, the
    latter proof, balance red and uncirculated   9 pieces

FIVE CENTS. NICKEL. 1866 to 1876, inclusive. '82 and
    '83 (2), uncirculated ; 1872 proof.   16 pieces

1867, '69, and '73. Proofs.   3 pieces

1143 THREE CENTS. NICKEL. 1865–1875, lacking '73: 1872 and '74 proof: balance uncirculated. 10 pieces

1144 1869, '74, and '75. Proofs. 3 pieces

1145 HARD TIMES TOKENS. Includes the " Big bellied donkey," " A friend to the constitution," also a number of early store cards. No duplicates; a fine lot. 36 pieces

1146 Jackson in money chest. Rev. Donkey: L.L. D. THE CONSTITUTION AS I UNDERSTAND IT, etc. *Brass:* fine.

1147 Hard times tokens. Duplicates. Good to fine. 34 pcs

1148 Feuchtwanger's composition. 1837. Arms of New York. Rev. THREE CENTS in wreath. Uncirculated : scarce.

1149 Duplicate. Very good.

1150 Feuchtwanger cent. 1837. Uncirculated.

COLONIAL COINS.

1151 Massachusetts. 1652. Oak tree shilling : split trunk variety. Small planchet : good.

1152 1652 Oak tree sixpence. Fine : very scarce.

1153 1652 Pine tree shilling. Small planchet : tree with bare, nearly straight and thick branches. Very good.

1154 1652 Pine tree shilling. Small planchet. Very good.

1155 1787 Cent. Very fair.

1156 1787 Half cent. Very good.

1157 1788 Cents. From different dies. Very good. 2 pcs

1158 Rosa Americana. 1723. Twopence. Bust of George I. Rev. Crowned rose. Nearly fine : very scarce.

1159 1722 Penny. Rev. Blooming rose uncrowned. Brass : very good.

1160 1722 Penny, from different dies. Copper : very good.

1161 1723 Penny. Rev Blooming rose crowned. Nearly fine ; scarce.

1162 1722 Halfpenny (farthing size). 1722. Rev. Blooming rose. Good ; very scarce.

1163 Colonies Françaises. 1767 Cent. Counterstamped R. F. Fine ; scarce.

1164 Virginia. 1773. Halfpenny. Sharp impression. Bright red.

1165 1773 Duplicate. Same condition.

1166 Nova Constellatio. 1788 and '85. Roman and script.
Good. 2 pieces

1167 1785 U. S. Rev. Short, blunt rays. Very good, and
struck on an unusually large planchet. 1R.

1168 Vermont. 1786. Cent. Rising sun over hills, dotted
with eight trees. VERMONTENSIUM RES PUBLICA, a
plough below. Rev. QUARTA DECIMA STELLA. Radiant eye surrounded by thirteen stars. Unusually
fine ; rare.

1169 1786 Cent. Same type. Nine trees on the hills. Very
good; scarce.

1170 1788 Vermon Auctori. Rev. Inde et Lib. From different dies. Fine ; very scarce. 5 pieces

1171 Confederatio. 1785. Rev. "Americana immies tyrannis."
Bolen's dies. A very close copy. Uncirculated.

1172 Georgius triumpho. 1788. Cent. Good ; dark.

1173 New York. 1787. Cent. NOVA EBORAC. Rev. Liberty
seated to left. Good ; scarce.

1174 1787 Immunis Columbia. Goddess of Liberty seated
with flag and scales. Rev. Eagle displayed. Very
good, and scarce.

1175 Fugio cent. 1787. "United States." Slender links in
chain. Fine olive color, uncir. Possibly a restrike.

1176 "States United" and "United States." Fair. 4 pieces

1177 U. S. A. or Bar cent. Original ; extremely fine. Rare.

1178 Kentucky cent. Pyramid of 15 stars, each inscribed
with initial letter of a State. Rev. Hand with scroll.
OUR CAUSE IS JUST. etc. Thin planchet ; uncir.
Very scarce.

1179 Talbot, Allum & Lee. N. Y., 1794. Cent. From different rev. dies. Very fine. 2 pieces

1180 The same. 1795. Cent. Uncirculated ; scarce.

1181 Pitt token. 1766. THE RESTORER OF COMMERCE. NO
STAMPS. Rev. Ship, AMERICA. etc. Fine. 1R.

1182 Duplicate of last number, and very nearly as fine as.

1183 Wood token. 1725. Rev. HIBERNIA. Fine. 1I.

1184 Vive pouni. 1760. Georgius III cis. etc. Poor and
fair. 4 pieces

1185 CONNECTICUT CENTS. 1786. Bust to left. AUCTORI
CONNEC. Rev. Liberty seated. INDE ETLIB. Very
good for this rare variety.

1186 1785. Head to right. From different dies. Fair to very
good ; all scarce. 6 pieces

1187 1786 Head to left. From different dies. Very good and scarce.   2 pieces

1188 1786 Head to right. Rev. ET LIB INDE. Very good; sc.

1189 1787 Mailed bust to left. From different dies. Good to fine. A rare lot.   5 pieces

1190 1787 Draped bust to left. Includes "Auctopi" and other scarce varieties. All from different dies. Average fine for this coinage.   13 pieces

1191 1788 Head to left. From different dies. Good and very good.   5 pieces

1192 1788 Head to right. Varieties; very good.   2 pieces

1193 1787 Smiling effigy, struck twice on obverse; 1788, so-called Washington head to right, struck over a "Nova Constellatio." Very good.   2 pieces

1194 Date poor or invisible; includes AUCTOPI. One pierced. Poor or fair.   7 pieces

1195 NEW JERSEY CENTS. 1786. Horse-head to right, a plough beneath. NOVA CAESAREA. Rev. U. S. shield, E. PLURIBUS UNUM. The mouth and breast of horse connected by a break in the die. Very fine: but small piece of edge wanting. A rare variety.

1196 1786 From different dies. One fine, 6 very good. A rare lot.   7 pieces

1197 1787 Large planchet. Fine and very scarce.

1198 1787 Large planchet. From different dies; very good.   2 pieces

1199 1787 Small horse-head and small plough with knobbed handles. Dark, even color; uncirculated.

1200 1787 Small plough: a crack in die through shield. Fine.

1201 1787 From different dies; includes very scarce varieties. Good and very good; a desirable lot.   12 pieces

1202 1788 Horse-head to left. Very fair: rare variety.

WASHINGTON MEDALS.

1203 The Eccleston Medal. Bust in armor to right. GENERAL WASHINGTON. Rev. Indian with bow and arrow, THE LAND WAS OURS, and inscription in three circular lines. Bronze; a perfect impression of this beautiful medal. Very fine and rare. 43.

1204 Laureated bust to right. METROPOLITAN CARNIVAL FEBRUARY 20 & 21, 1871. Rev. View of the Capitol at Washington and inscription in twelve lines. Lead; very fine and rare. 47.

1205 Washington before Boston. Naked bust to right, by Du Vivier. Rev. View of the evacuation. Bronze, extremely fine. 48.

1206 Another. Tin or lead, and a copper shell or electro of the obverse. Good and fine. 2 pieces

1207 Centennial, 1876. Bust to left. Rev. The Cherry Tree scene, "I cannot tell a lie." *Hard*, in three shades of color. 38. 3 pieces

1208 Naked bust to right, by *Paquet*. Rev. Bust on pedestal. WASHINGTON CABINET OF MEDALS. U. S. MINT. INAUGURATED FEB. 22. 1860. *Silver*; proof. 38.

1209 The same. Bronze proof. 38.

1210 Naked bust to right, by *Lovett, Phila*. Rev. Minerva seated. NATUS FEB. XXII. MDCCXXXII., etc. White metal, proof. 33.

1211 Same obverse. Rev., TO COMMEMORATE THE HUNDREDTH ANNIVERSARY, etc. 1876. White metal; proof. 33.

1212 Centennial Medal. Bust of Washington in oval, crowned by cupids. MDCCLXXVI. above. Rev. Four female figures grouped around Columbia. INTERNATIONAL EXHIBITION, 1876. The Copenhagen Medal. Bronze, brilliant proof. 28.

1213 Same design, but LET US HAVE PEACE above. Bronze, brilliant proof. 38.

1214 Duplicates of two last Nos. White m. proof. 2 pieces

1215 Naked bust to right, by Laubenheimer. FIRST IN WAR, etc., star above, square and compasses below. Rev. The Cherry Tree scene. All-seeing eye and G. W. above. MAGNA EST VERITAS ET PREVALEBIT. I CANNOT TELL A LIE. 1776. Copper, proof. 34.

1216 The same. Yellow bronze and w. m.; proof. 34. 2 pieces

1217 Naked bust to left. GEORGE WASHINGTON, UNITED STATES OF AMERICA. Broad ornamental border, eagle with flag above. Rev. View of Crystal Palace, New York, 1853. Bronze; very fine and scarce. 34.

1218 Head to right. Eagle with streamer, stars and angles on broad border. Rev. Ground floor of Masonic temple. MDCCCLIX. Bronze; extremely fine. 34.

1219 The same. Yellow bronze and w. m. Proof. 2 pieces

1220 Same obv. Rev. View of Washington's statue, Union Square, N. Y. MDCCCLXI. Very fine. 34.

1221 Naked bust to right. GEORGE WASHINGTON FIRST PRESIDENT OF THE U. S. A. MDCCLXXXIX. Rev. Wreath. AWARDED TO White metal; fine. 42.

1222 Bust in uniform to left. Names of Presidents to M. Van Buren, dates of death, etc. Rev. Eagle with flag and scroll inscribed ALL MEN ARE CREATED EQUAL, 1776. 1846 in exergue. Tin ; bronzed. Fine for this scarce medal. 32.

1223 Busts of eight Presidents, Washington in the centre. Rev. Names in broad wreath of flowers. Tin : unc. 30.

1224 Same obv. Rev. BUCHANAN (a buck and a cannon) AND BRECKENRIDGE in starry field. Bronze : unc. 30.

1225 Naked bust to right by *Key.* THE FARMER OF MOUNT VERNON. Rev. Engraved. Award medal of the Lancaster Co. Agricultural and Mechanical Society. 1858. *Silver ;* extremely fine. 28.

1226 Bust to right. Rev. Fasces, sword, and wreath on altar, COMMIS RESIGNED : PRESIDENCY RELINQUISHED 1797. Bronze proof. 28.

1227 Naked bust to left 1776-1876. Rev. Females with shields, etc., the Exhibition buildings in the distance. SEE HOW WE PROSPER. White metal, proof. 28.

1228 Small bust to left. THE UNION MUST AND SHALL BE PRESERVED 1856, etc., in two circular lines. Rev. Same as rev. of No. 1224. W. m.: nearly proof. 29.

1229 Large head to left. GEORGE WASHINGTON. Rev. BORN FEB 22D 1732, CHOSEN COMMANDER IN CHIEF, JULY 1776, CHOSEN PREST 1789, DIED DECR 14 1799, AGED 68 YEARS | in wreath. Bronze : fine. 28.

1230 Same obv. Rev. Blank. White metal : fine. 28.

1231 Bust of Washington on pedestal inscribed 1776–1876, saluted by a veteran and a private of the 7th Regt. N. G. S. N. Y. Rev. Arms and trophy. Centennial medal, to commemorate the visit of the 7th Regt. to Philadelphia, 1876. *Silver ;* proof. 28.

1232 The same. Bronze and white metal ; proof.   2 pieces

1233 Female crowning the bust of Washington. Rev Benevolence relieving distress. *Silver* medal of the Washington Benevolent Society, 1808. Loop removed. w. H. A. D. engraved on field. Fine. 26.

1234 Naked bust to right. Rev. WE AGREE TO ABSTAIN, &c. Washington Temperance Society medal. Brass and w. m. Fine. 26.   2 pieces

1235 Same obv. Rev. HOUSE OF TEMPERANCE. Bronze : fine. 26.

1236 Bust to right. Rev. Fasces, sword, and wreath on altar, COMMIS RESIGNED. PRESIDENCY RELINQ 1797. *Silver ;* proof. 26.

1237 The same. Bronze; extremely fine. 26.

1238 Bust to right by *Westwood*. Rev. Wreath dotted with 13 stars, 13 arrows above. MADE COMMANDER IN CHIEF OF THE AMERICAN FORCES, etc. Bronze; extremely fine. 26.

1239 Naked bust to right. THE FATHER OF HIS COUNTRY. Rev. Monument. Wh. m. pierced. Fine. 24.

1240 Naked bust to right; panels with troops of cavalry and infantry on border. TO COMMEMORATE THE 100TH ANNIVERSARY, etc. Rev. View of the signing of Declaration of Independence; from Trumbull's painting. *Silver*; proof. 28.

1241 The same. Thick pl. Bronze; fine. 28.

1242 Same obv. Rev. Signature of Hancock. W. m.; pr. 28.

1243 California Centennial Medal. 1776–1876. Small bust of Washington in wreath over landscape, showing progress made in the settlement of the State, etc. Loop; thick planchet. *Silver*; proof. 23.

1244 The same. Thin planchet, without loop. *Silver*; proof. 23.

1245 Another. Tin, silvered; loop. Proof.

1246 Busts jugata of Washington and Franklin to left. Rev. Eagle hovering over a section of globe inscribed *United States*. 1783 above. Bronze; extremely fine. 25.

1247 Bust nearly facing. Rev. A MAN HE WAS TO ALL HIS COUNTRY DEAR in wreath. All-seeing eye above. W. m.; proof. 24.

1248 Centennial Medals. 1876. Includes the California; no other duplicates of last Nos., and all different. W. m. Two pierced; proof. 24 to 26.   7 pieces

1249 Military bust to right. Rev. INDEPENDENCE HALL. 1776. 1876. W. m.; proof. 24.

1250 Large head to left. Rev. PRESENTED BY THE METROPOLITAN MECHANICS INSTITUTE; name engraved. Bronze; fine. 24.

1251 Large bust to right. Rev. FREE AND UNITED STATES. 1876. Copper and brass, proof. 24.   2 pieces

1252 Bust of Washington to left. N. & G. Taylor Co.'s Philadelphia card. Three varieties, brass +3, and white metal. All fine and scarce. 24.   5 pieces

1253 Bust of Washington. Rev. Merchants die; gone. Rather fine and rare. 23.

1254 Full figure of Washington, a horse behind him. Rev. calendar. Brass; fine. 25.

1255 Washington on horseback. Brass, calendar : uncir. 21.

1256 Naked bust to right, surrounded by 34 stars. THE CEN-
TENNIAL YEAR OF OUR NATIONAL INDEPENDENCE.
Rev. Blazing star inscribed 1776, and names of en-
gagements fought in 1776, numbered 1 to 8. *Silver,*
proof : rare and complete set. 22. 8 pieces

1257 Another set. Bronze ; perfect. 8 pieces

1258 Small bust in wreath of palm and oak. 100TH ANNI-
VERSARY OF THE DECLARATION OF INDEPENDENCE,
JULY 4, 1876. Rev. Same as last. Bronze : perfect
and very rare. 8 pieces

1259 Bust in toga to right. Rev. Washington's residence at
Mount Vernon. Copper : proof. 22.

1260 Duplicates. Cop. and w. m. ; proof. 2 pieces

1261 Bust nearly facing. UNITY OF GOVERNMENT IS THE
MAIN PILLAR OF INDEPENDENCE. Rev. HE IS A
FREEMAN WHOM THE TRUTH MAKES FREE. *Silver :*
nearly proof. Rare. 22.

1262 The same. Tin, proof. 22.

1263 Bust nearly facing. 1732–1799. Rev. Coat of Arms of
Washington. *Harzfeld's Series.* W. m. : proof. 21.

1264 Small medallion bust suspended to eagle's beak. Rev.
STRUCK AND DISTRIBUTED IN CIVIC PROCESSION,
FEB. 22ND. 1832, etc. *Silver ;* nearly proof. 20.

1265 The same. Bronze ; thick pl. Perfect. 20.

1266 The same. Tin ; thin and thick pl. Uncir. 2 pieces

1267 Washington on horseback to left. Rev. SIEGE OF
BOSTON in wreath. Cop. br. and w. m. ; proof. 20.
3 pieces

1268 Same obv., but GEO WASHINGTON 1776 above. Rev.
Same, with the addition of *Lovett's Series,* *No.* 2.
Phila. Silver : nearly proof. 20.

1269 The same. Bronze, copper and brass. Nearly pr. • 20.
3 pieces

1270 Naked bust to right in wreath of palm branches. Rev.
WASHINGTON in radiant sun, surrounded by 13 stars.
Bronze, proof 20.

1271 Long bust in military uniform to left. GEORGE WASH-
INGTON, THE CINCINNATUS OF AMERICA. B. 1732.
D. 1799. Rev. THE UNION MUST AND SHALL BE
PRESERVED, in circle of stars. *Silver,* proof 20.

1272 Same obv. Rev. "John K. Curtis " card. Copper,
proof. 20.

1273 Small bust of Washington in keystone. 1732-1799.
Rev. FIT KEYSTONE IN THE TRIUMPHAL ARCH WHICH
SPANS THE NATION'S CENTURY. Designed by Isaac
F. Wood. Copper, proof. 30.

1274 Oath of allegiance medal. Naked bust to right by
Paquet. Rev. Inscription in wreath. Thick planchet; *silver*, proof. 19.

1275 Another. Thin planchet; *silver*. proof. 19.

1276 The same. Thick and thin planchet. Bronze, proof.
19.   2 pieces

1277 Same obverse. Rev. Plain laurel wreath, no inscription. *Silver*, proof. 19.

1278 Naked bust to right. GEORGE WASHINGTON SECURITY.
Rev. PRO PATRIA in wreath. Copper; proof. 24.

1279 Naked bust to right. GEORGE WASHINGTON. Rev.
BORN FEB 1732 DIED DEC 14 1799. *Silver*, proof.
20.

1280 The same. Bronze, cop. and w. m. Very fine.   3 ps

1281 Same obverse. Rev. Edward Cogan's card. Cop. and
w. m. Very fine. 20   2 pcs

1282 Bust in toga to right. GEORGE WASHINGTON. Rev.
PRO PATRIA in wreath (3), and monument at Balto.
Bronze, copper, and w. m. Very fine. 56.   4 pieces

1283 Naked bust to right. GEORGE WASHINGTON. BORN
FEBRUARY 22, 1732. Rev. Tomb; DIED DECEMBER
14, 1799. RESURGEMUS. Bronze, copper, and w.
m. (silvered). Very fine. 20.   3 pieces

1284 Same obverse. Rev. Bust of Everett. Bronze and
copper; very fine. 20.   2 pieces

1285 Same obverse. Rev. Bust of Franklin. Bronze and
w. m. Very fine. 20.   2 pieces

1286 Same obverse. Rev. "John Thompson corporal Co I,
Harris 1st cav Oswego N. Y.," etc. engraved. W m.;
pierced. Rare. 20. 19.

1287 Bust to left. 1776-1876. 100TH YEAR OF OUR
NATIONAL INDEPENDENCE. Rev. 45TH ANNIVERSARY
OF THE BROOKLYN SUNDAY SCHOOL UNION, MAY, 1876.
Copper, brass, and w. m. Proof. 8 pieces.

1288 Bust of Lincoln to left. 1864. Rev. Small head of
Washington on five-pointed star. UNION. FREEDOM
TO ALL MEN. Bronze, brass, and w. m. Very fine.
30.   5 pieces

1289 Miscellaneous. Each with bust of Washington, and
different. W m. One pierced; all extremely fine.
20 to 22.   8 pieces

1290 Small bust to left. by *Bolen*. George Washington. Rev.
AVOID THE EXTREMES OF PARTY SPIRIT in wreath of
oak. Bronze : proof. 18.

1291 Short bust to right. GEORGE WASHINGTON. Rev.
TIME INCREASES HIS FAME. Bronze ; thick and thin
pl. Extremely fine.   2 pieces

1292 Busts nearly facing of Washington and Franklin. Rev.,
small busts in wreath, and PAR NOBILE FRATRUM.
Cop., brass, and w. m. ; proof. 17.   4 pieces

1293 Small busts facing. Rev. PAR NOBILE FRATRUM in
wreath. Nickel, cop., and w. m. ; proof. 17.   3 pieces

1294 Military bust to left, by *Bolen*. Rev. SOLDIERS' FAIR,
SPRINGFIELD, MASS., DEC. 1864. W. m.; uncirculated.
18.

1295 Bust to left in arch by *Key*. 1732 PATRIAE PATER.
Rev. Bust of Webster, Forrest, also "Dedicated to
coin & medal collectors." Cop. and w. m. ; very fine.
17.   3 pieces

1296 Bust to left by *Key*. PATRIAE PATER. 1732. Rev.
Cupid on dolphin, Virtue. Liberty and Independence,
" Providence left him childless," etc, etc. Bronze
and copper ; nearly proof. 18.   3 pieces

1297 The same. White metal, proof.   3 pieces

1298 Small head of Washington over a starry cloud in trophy
of flags. THE UNION MUST AND SHALL BE PRE-
SERVED. Rev. All different. Brass (1), and w. m. ;
proof.   6 pieces

1299 Bust of Washington. M. A. ABRAHAMS. Rev. WES-
TON MO. Brass, fine. 17.

1300 Military bust to left. Rev. Views of Headquarters.
Nos. 1 to 9 complete. Copper ; proof. 17.   9 pcs.

1301 Same obverse. Rev. BORN FEB. 22ND, 1732. etc. Cop.,
brass, and w. m. : proof. 18.   3 pieces

1302 Same obverse. Rev. Andrew Jackson on horseback.
Cop., brass, and w. m. ; proof. 18.   3 pieces

1303 Same obverse. Rev. Bust of Harrison. Cop., brass,
and w m. ; proof. 18.   3 pieces

1304 Same obverse. Rev. Bust of Henry Clay. Cop., brass,
and w. m.; proof. 18.   3 pieces

1305 Washington on horseback, to right. GEORGE WASH-
INGTON. Rev. Jackson on horseback, to left. Cop.,
brass, and w. m. ; proof. 18.   3 pieces

1306 Same obverse. Rev. Bust of Harrison. Copper and
brass; proof. 18.   2 pieces

1807 Same obverse. Rev. Bust of Henry Clay. Cop., brass. and w. m.; proof. 18. 3 pieces

1808 Military bust to left. TO AID ST. JOHN'S GUILD FLOAT-ING HOSPITAL (*Wood's Series*, "C" *No.* 5). Rev. Bust of Martha W. CENTENNIAL RECEPTION, BALL AND TEA PARTY, ACADEMY OF MUSIC, N. Y., FEB. 22, 1876. *Silver;* proof, and extremely rare. 18.

1809 Naked bust to left. THE PATTERN OF PATRIOTISM, IN-DUSTRY AND PROGRESS. Rev. UNION AGRICULTURAL SOC. OF RIDGEWAY AND SHELBY, N. Y., ORGANIZED JULY 17, 1858. *Silver;* proof, very rare. 18.

1810 Cloaked bust to left in wreath of laurel. WASHINGTON THE FATHER OF OUR COUNTRY. Rev. Trophy of shield and flags. THE BOYS AND GIRLS OF AMERICA, 1876. Cop. and brass; proof. 18. 2 pieces

1811 Naked bust to right. Rev. WASHINGTON BORN, 1732, DIED 1799, in wreath. *Silver;* proof. 18.

1812 The same. Copper; very fine.

1813 Naked bust to right, as before. GEORGE WASHINGTON and G. H. L. in exergue. Rev. Square and compasses. INIT IN FREDERICKSBURGH LODGE NO. 4 VIRGINIA NOV. 4 1752. *Silver;* proof. 18.

1814 The same. Copper and brass; proof. 2 pieces

1815 Short bust to right. FIRST IN WAR, etc. Rev. Bust of Lincoln. REVERSE LINCOLN and 12 stars. Cop. and w. m.; uncirculated. 18. 2 pieces

1816 Duplicates, etc. 1 brass, 7 w. m.; fine, 4 pierced. 18. 8 pieces

1817 Bust of Martha Washington to left. THE 100TH YEAR, etc. Rev. MARTHA WASHINGTON MEMORIAL MEDAL on label. Cop., brass and w. m.; proof. 17. 3 pcs

1818 Spiel marks, bust of Washington. Brass; a fine lot; large and small. 18 pieces

1819 Short bust to right, in broad wreath. WASHINGTON, M. in exergue. Rev. THE HERO, etc. (?), and Jas. H. Merriam's card. Bronze, copper, brass, and w. m. Very fine. 17. 5 pieces

1820 Bust to right by *Bolen.* WASHINGTON. Rev. THE UNION IS THE MAIN PROP, etc. Cop. and brass, proof. 16. 2 pieces

1821 Draped bust to right. GEN'L GEORGE WASHINGTON FIRST PRES U. S. 1789. Rev. Shield, and E. Ivin's card. Nickel, copper, brass and w. m. Very fine. 16. 4 pieces

1822 The same. *Silver;* very fine.

1323 Same obv. Rev. Arm in square and compasses o. u. a. m. Silvered and brass; fine. 2 pieces

1324 Small head to right. N & G TAYLOR CO 1863 PHILADELPHIA. Thick pl., cop. Very fine. 16.

1325 Small head in wreath to right. *Bale.* WASHINGTON TEMPERANCE BENEVOLENT SOCIETY. Rev. WE SERVE TYRANT ALCOHOL NO LONGER. *Silver;* pierced, un-cir. 13.

1326 Bust to right. Rev. GREAT FAIR NANTUCKET MASS AUGUST 1864 Brass; good and scarce. 15.

1327 Bust to left. WASHINGTON, etc. Rev. TO THE CAUSE OF TEMPERANCE TEN DOLLARS, etc. Brass; fine. 15. 2 pieces

1328 Large head to left. GEORGES WASHINGTON. *Pezut* (?) under the bust. Rev. Blank. Brass; silvered. No doubt very rare; not in Wood's collection. 14.

1329 Naked bust to left. Rev. Monument at Baltimore. Copper, brass, and w. m. Uncirculated. 12. 4 pcs

1330 Bust to right. GEORGE WASHINGTON. Rev. Bust of Martha W. (3) and W. Idler's card. Nickel, copper, and brass. Very fine. 13. 4 pieces

1331 Bust of Washington, nearly facing. *Bale* below. Rev. Bust of Franklin. *Silver,* copper, and w. m. Proof. 13. 3 pieces

1332 Bust to right. PATER PATRIAE. Rev. A MEMORIAL OF THE WASHINGTON CABINET, MAY 1859. *Silver* and bronze; proof. 14. 3 pieces

1333 Bust to left. PATER PATRIAE. Rev. Varieties of Sage's card. Copper; uncirculated. 12. 2 pieces

1334 Naked bust to right. Rev. "Born 1732," etc.; Jackson. Lincoln, square and compasses. *Silver;* fine to proof, one pierced. 12. 4 pieces

1335 Same obverse. Rev. "Born. 1732." etc. Grant. Centennial bell, and square and compasses. Bronze, copper, and brass. Uncirculated. 12. 4 pieces

1336 Smaller bust in uniform to right. Rev. "Born, 1732," etc. Bronze and copper. Uncirculated. 11. 3 pcs

1337 Bust to right. Rev. GREAT CENTRAL FAIR, PHILADELPHIA, JUNE, 1864. *Silver* and copper. Fine. 11. 2 pieces

1338 Bust to left. REPRESENTED BY WM. LEGGETT BRAMHALL. Nick., cop., etc. Very fine. 12. 4 pieces.

1339 Miscellaneous. All different. Bronze, copper, nickel, etc., 2 pierced. A fine lot. 11 to 16. 15 pieces.

1340 Bust to left. Rev. Radiant star. *Silver*, uncir., rare. 6.
1341 Bust to right. Rev. Blank. *Silver* ; pierced. Uncirculated, rare. 6.

WASHINGTON COINS.

1342 1783 Cent. Bust laureate to left. Rev. UNITY STATES.
Very fine.

1343 1783 Duplicate ; also double-head cent and rev. UNITED
STATES. Very fair. 3 pieces

1344 Washington and Independence. Rev. UNITED STATES.
Bronze proof. Probably restruck in England about
1863.

1345 The same. Bronze and copper proofs. 2 pieces

1346 1791 Cent. Military bust to left. WASHINGTON PRESI-
DENT. Rev. Small eagle. Uncir. ; very scarce.

1347 1791 Cent. Large eagle reverse. Proof.

1348 1793 Liverpool halfpenny. Military bust to left and
ship. Lettered edge ; very fine.

1349 (1795) Military bust to left. GEORGE WASHINGTON.
Rev. Eagle on shield. LIBERTY AND SECURITY. " An
asylum for the oppressed of all nations " on edge.
Copper ; uncirculated. 24.

1350 1795 Military bust to right. GEORGE WASHINGTON.
Rev. Similar to last, date below. Copper ; lettered
edge. Very fine. 18.

1351 1795 Bust to right. Rev. A grate. Engrailed edge.
Very fine and scarce. 18.

1352 Success to the United States. Large and small. Brass ;
good. 2 pieces

AMERICAN STORE CARDS.

A most extensive and complete collection, containing very many of the
earlier and rarer issues and others quite before issued of service. To
save endless repetitions, I will state that, unless otherwise specified, store
cards or business tokens are uniserved, and in medium average
time very fine is understood. Also that there are to duplicate if few,
and in lots only duplicates in different metal.

1353 AMSDEN, N. C. Genoa, Ill. 1845. Copper. 17.

1354 Abrahams, M. A. Weston, Mo, (2 varieties), Independence, the latter poor. Brass. 17. 3 pieces

1355 Adams. Rev. 1817. Copper. 12.

1356 Atwood's (electro), Ashton. Applegates, Aldridge & Earp, Alexander, Amer. Life Ins. Co., Henry Anderson, Angue, Apollo Gardens, Adams. Copper, brass, and white metal, one pierced. 14 to 18.   15 pieces

1357 **B**ARNETT, Newark. N. J. Iron; cast. 22.

1358 Becks. Public Baths, Richmond. Nude female figure. Nickel. 18.

1359 The same. Copper. 18.

1360 Bridesburg. Barrel Manf. Co. Rev. Blank. Brass. 20.

1361 Benson, J. J. 50 (tin) and 10 (brass) cents. 12 and 17.   2 pieces

1362 Buchan, David C. New York. Brass. 17.

1363 Burbank & Shaw. Chicago, 1847. Copper. 16.

1364 Bailey & Co., 819 Chestnut St., Phila. *Silver.* 18.

1365 The same. Brass and plated.   2 pieces

1366 Baker, Wright & Howard (poor), Baker & Moody, Baker & Co., Bull & Co., Barcley, Barker & Illsley, Barnum, Barton & Co., Bassett & Co., Beals, Benedict & Burnham, Benziger Bros., Bergen Iron Works, B F Z & CO. Nickel, cop., br. and w. m., one pierced. 12 to 24.   20 pieces

1367 Black, Samuel H. & Samuel N. (electros), Blakely, Bliss, Blue Stone, Bolen, Bollenhagen & Comp., Boston Whist, Bowen & McNamee. Cop., brass, w. m., tin. 14 to 26.   20 pieces

1368 Bradstreet Hoffman & Co., Bramhall, Breed & Fursman, Brigham, Brimelow, Brown, Brooks (25 c.), Brown & Brothers (3, pierced), Browning Brothers, Bucklins, Burr & Witsil, Budd (pierced), Burwell, Byrneore Gold, Byron & Co. Silver (1), cop., br., w. m. and rubber (1). 12 to 22.   30 pieces

1369 Brigham, Francis D., New Bedford, 1833. Copper; uncir. 18.

1370 **C**ATCH CLUB. 12½ CENTS. Rev. Shield and stars. Brass. 18.

1371 Cogan, Edward. Nickel, bronze, copper and w. m. 13 to 19.   6 pieces

1372 Clinton Lunch. Brass. 12.

1373 Cornell Watch Co., San Francisco. Nickel, cop., gilt, etc. 19.   5 pieces

1374 Cossitt, Hill & Co., Memphis. 8 different reverses, including "Wealth of the South," and "No Submission to the North." Cop. and brass. 14.   11 pieces

1375 Currier & Greeley, Boston, Mass. Cop. 17.

1376 Campbell, Carrington & Co., Chamberlain Woodruff &
Scranton, Cheseborough Stearns & Co., Chadwick,
Citizens' Line, City Coal Yard, Clark's (10c.), Clark
& Anthony, Cleaves, Cole, Colgate & Co. Nickel,
cop., brass and w. m. 12 to 20. 17 pieces

1377 Chapman, W. B. Varieties. Nickel. 12. 5 pieces

1378 Cook, Countiss, Crossman, Curtis. Cop., br. and w. m.
12 to 26. 13 pieces

1379 **D**ADMAN & CO., 15 Court Square. Rev. "Massachusetts Eating House." Lead. 16.

1380 Day, Newell & Day, 589 Broadway, New York, W & B.
N. Y. Copper. 17.

1381 Dickson White & Co., Philadelphia. Cop. and brass.
18. 2 pieces

1382 Draper & Sandland, Attleboro. Mass. Calendar. Brass,
silvered. 25.

1383 Durfee, E. H., "Good for one dollar in merchandise."
Rev. Indian on horseback. Brass. 17.

1384 Davenport, Davidson, Daytons, Defandorf, Depuy, De-
veau, Diehl, Dimmick, Dobbins, Dodd, Doll & Co.,
Dorman's, Dorrans & Nixon, Drown & Co., Duncan,
Dunn & Co., Durkee & Co. Nickel, cop., brass and
w. m., one pierced. 11 to 18. 34 pieces

1385 Dickeson. Coin Safe. Rev Summer Islands and bust
of Washington. Nickel, cop, brass and w. m. 26.
5 pieces

1386 **E**LLIOTT, Vinson & Co., Memphis. Six different
reverses, including "No Submission to the North"
and "The Wealth of the South." Copper and br.
14. 7 pieces

1387 Eastman, Eckstein, Edwards, Elgin Na. Watch Co.,
Erwin, Esterbrook & Co., Eureka Co., Evans &
Allen, Evans & Watson, Evans, Exchange. Nickel,
cop., br. and w. m. 12 to 20. 16 pieces

1388 **F**ARMERS and Mechanics Life Ins. Co., N. Y. Rev.
"One Hundred Thousand Dollars Dep." silver. 14

1389 Farnsworth, Phipps & Co. Boston. W & B. mint
border. Copper. 17.

1390 Feuchtwanger. Eagle on a rock. 1837. Rev. 3.
THREE CENTS in wreath of oak. FEUCHTWANGER'S
COMPOSITION. Proof. 15. One of this type, not as
fine, sold in one of my sales at $30.00.

/. 2) 1391 Coat of arms of New York. 1837. Rev. THREE CENTS in wreath of laurel. FEUCHTWANGERS COMPOSITION. Very fine. 15.

) 1392 Eagle grasping snake. Rev. 3 THREE cents in wreath of oak. FEUCHTWANGERS COMPOSTION. Uncirculated. 15.

1393 Feuchtwanger Cents. From different dies. 3 pieces

1394 Fox's Casino. Phila. Cop. 12.

1395 Frank's. Rev. 25 SUTLER'S GOODS. Brass. 13.

1396 Farmers & Mechanics, Fargason Cordes & Co., Fera, F. H. F. Co. (pierced), Finck's, Fisk (pierced), Fitnam, Jr. (pierced), Fitzgibbon, Flagg, Flagg & Macdonald, Flanagan. Fobes & Barlow, Folger. Copper, br., w. m. 12 to 19. 22 pieces

5 1397 Foster & Parry, Foster Martin & Co., Foster & Metcalf, Foterall, Fountain Blacking, Francisco & Co., Francisco & Whitman, Fredericks, Freedman Goodkind and Co., Friend & Black (electro), Fries, Malseed & Hawkins, Frisbie, Fussell. Copper, brass, and w. m. 12 to 17. 25 pieces

1398 GIBBS, W. N. Y. Rev. Cow, "A friend to the Constitution." 17.

1399 Grimshaw, W. D. New York. W. m. 24.

1400 Gustin & Blake, Chelsea, Vt. Copper. 18.

1401 Gaffney, Gage, Lyall & Keeler (pierced), Gustin & Blake, Gates & Trask, Geissler (pierced), Gentlemens Furnishing Store, J. H. & J. Henry Gercke, Gerts, Gilmore (pierced), Globe Fire Ins. Co. (pierced), Good for a ride, Goodrich & Gay, Goulds Saloon, Gowans & Co., Green & Wetmore, Gunther. 12 to 18. 23 pieces

1402 HALLOCK, Dolson & Bates, New York. Copper and brass. 18. 2 pieces

1403 Hallock & Bates, New York. Cop. 18.

1404 Hardie, A. W. New York. Rev. "Naked, and ye clothed me." Copper. 20.

1405 Hansman, W. H. Savannah, Geo. Brass. 14.

1406 Hörter, Charles D. New York. Copper. 16.

1407 Houghton, Merrell & Co. N. Y. Brass. 17.

1408 Howell Works Garden. A rose, Rev. Token. Cop. 17.

1409 Ditto. A grape. Rev. SIGNUM 1834. 14.

1410 Hyde, J. B. . 1853 and '54. Cop. and brass calendars. 21 and 25. 2 pieces

- 1411 Hamill & Co., Hammett & Cheseldine. Hand, Handy, Harbach, Harmstead. Hurts, Hart & Co., Hazelton & Palmer, Haskins, Hathaway, Havens, Heilbroner, Henning, Herschenau, Hess & Speidel, Dr. J. G. Hewett, T. Hoag, Hodgman, Holden & Co., Helmus Booth & Haydens, H. W. Hoops, Hopkins, Hughes House, Huyler, Howe Machine. Copper, br., w. m. and (1) rubber. 12 to 24. 56 pieces

— 1412 Hill, E., New York. 8 different reverses. Cop., brass, and w. m. 18. 17 pieces

1413 **IVINS**, E., Philadelphia. *Silver.* 16.

1414 The same. Nickel, cop., br. and w. m. 14 & 16. 5 pieces

1415 Idler, W. *Silver* (1), nickel, cop., and br. 13. 12 pieces

1416 The same. Cop., br., and w. m. 21. 5 pieces

1417 **JENSCH**, F. A., Chicago. Copper (2), and bronze. 15. 3 pieces

1418 Jones, Wm. G., New York. Br.; pierced and plugged. 17.

1419 J. P. Rev. Eagle. Brass; fair only. 15.

1420 Judson, Hiram, Syracuse, N. Y. Cop., thick and thin pl. 17. 2 pieces

1421 Jaccard & Co., Jackson, Jacobs, James Clark & Co., Jarvis, Jefferson Ins. Co., Jenkins, Jennings Whitlier & Co., Professor & Prof. Johnson, J. H. T., Joseph Brothers. Cop., br., and w. m. 12 to 18. 33 pieces

1422 **KENNEDY**, S., Trenton, N. J. Rev. Slater, Walton & Co., Philada. Tin; proof. 14.

1423 Key. "Ornamental medal," etc. Rev. "We all have our hobbies." 12 different reverses. Cop., brass, and tin. 17. 13 pieces

1424 Key, F. C. & Sons, 129 & 329 Arch Street, Philad. 7 different reverses, inclusive of Woodgate & Co., N. Y. Copper, br., and w. m. 17. 7 pieces

1425 Head of Liberty. Rev. Wm. H. Key, J. H. Dohn, Philadelphia. Copper; proof. 14

1426 Key, F. C. & Sons, 329 Arch Street, Phila. "Reform of State flags of Penn. Regts." Brass. 24.

1427 **LAW**, H., New York. Copper. 18.

1428 Lee & Reynolds, Cheyenne agency. Rev. Buffalo. German silver. 29.

1429 Leech, J. N. T. Rev. Woodgate & Co., New York. 1860. *Silver*; proof. 17.

1430 The same. Cop., br., and w. m. 17. 3 pieces

1431 The same. 904 Broadway, New York, 1860. Rev. "No pleasure can exceed the smoking of the weed." White metal ; proof. 17.

1432 Lingg & Bro., Phila. 6 different reverses. Cop., br., and w. m. 14. 8 pieces

1433 Lingg & Co., Phila. Varieties of rev. Copper and w. m. 14. 5 pieces

1434 Loomis, A., Cleveland, Ohio. Rev., Fish, whisky, etc. Copper. 19.

1435 Lovett, R., Jr., Phila. 5 varieties. Bronze, nickel, cop., brass, and w. m. 9, 12, and 22. 16 pieces

1436 Lovett, R., New York. Rev. Bust of Franklin. *Silver :* proof. 17.

1437 The same. Cop. and brass. Proof. 2 pieces

1438 Kelly, Kendall, Kentucky Currency (Salt River Bourbon 2), Ketcham & Barker, Kilbride, Kingsley & Son, Kinsay, Kleinsteuber, Kline, Knapp, Knoppel, Cop., br., and w. m. 14 to 17. 26 pieces

1439 Lang, Leack, Leighton, Leverett & Thomas (poor), Link & Dannacher, Loder & Co., Long, E., and Wm. W., Lovett, Geo. H. & J. D., Luckey & Platt, Ludwig, Lyons & Co., Lyon. Copper, brass, white metal, etc. 14 to 20. 29 pieces

1440 MACY, R. H. & Co., New York. 1876. Copper, thick planchet. 17.

1441 Marshall, M. L., Oswego, N. Y. *Silver.* 17.

1442 Memphis Jockey Club. 1858. Oval brass badge, engraved. 32 x 40.

1443 Merle, John A. & Co., New Orleans. Rev. Genevese arms and motto. Copper. 17.

1444 Merritt & Langley's Dey St. House, New York. Rev. /6, /9, 1/6, 1/3, 1, 2, 2/9, 3/6. German silver. 20. 8 pieces

1445 Metropolitan Insurance Co., New York. 1852. Silver. 17.

1446 The same, 1852 ; another, "Capital 1.000.000," etc. Copper. 17 and 20. 2 pieces

1447 Miller, M. H. & Co., Memphis. *Silver.* 18.

1448 Milton, Wm. H., Boston. Varieties. Cop. 18. 2 pieces

1449 Moran & Clark, "Californian gold warranted," etc. Rev. "San Francisco, California," etc. Copper. 18.

1450 Moss' Hotel, New York. Rev. 6, 9d., 1/6, 1/9, 2, 2/9, 3/3, 3/6, 3/9, 4. Brass. 16. 10 pieces

1451 Muss' Hotel, New York. Rev. "Sweeny's Hotel," "Smithsonian House," "A. D. Thompson," blank. Copper and brass. 16. 6 pieces

1452 Mott's, New York, 1789. Copper. 16.

1453 Mullen, Wm. J., New York. Copper. 20.

1454 Machine shop, Magnus, Mahony's, Malcolm & Gaul, Malseed & Hawkins, March, Margarita, Marks & Co., M. L. Marshall, Mason & Co., Marston & Co. (50c.), Mathews, Maverick Coach, Maycock & Co., Meade & Bro., Mears & Hamilton. *Silver*, german silver, cop., brass, w. m., and lead. 11 to 20. 31 pieces

1455 Mechanics Savings Bank, Merchants Exchange, Jos. H. Merriam, Merriam & Co., Merritt, Miller & Co., Milliken's Hotel, Mitchel, Milton & Co., Mobile Jockey Club, Moffet, Morgan & Orr, Morris & Messinger, Morse's Literary Depot, "Most extensive in the U. S.," Murdock & Spencer, Mulligan. 11 to 21. Nickel, cop., and w. m. 31 pieces

1456 N. Y. & Harlaem R. R. Co. *H. & S. N. Y.* Nickel, octagonal. 12.

1456* Nicholson, New York Joint Stock Co., New Congress Hall, Needles, Navy Yard Route, National Elgin Watch Co. Nickel, cop., brass, w. m. 11 to 18. 7 pieces

1457 OLCOTT Brother, Omnibus Line, Oppenheimer & Metzger. Nickel, cop. and brass. 12 to 17. 5 pcs

1458 PARMELEE, Webster & Co. N. Y. Bust of Grant. *Silver*, cop., br., and w. m.; proof. 14. 4 pieces

1459 Peale, Charles Wilson, Founder, 1784. Rev. "Admit the bearer, Philadelphia Museum." Copper. 26.

1460 Peale's Museum, etc. Rev. "Parthenon, New York." 1825. Copper. 22.

1461 Percy, E. D., Troy, N. Y. Brass. 18.

1462 Person, Q. B., Calendars, 1855 and '56. Copper and w. m. 22. 2 pieces

1463 Potter, S., Newport. Brass. 18.

1464 Patapsco Fruit Butter Co., P. & Co., Patterson Bros., Pearson & Dann, Peck, J. & G., Peck's Depot, Peck & Burnham, Peirce, Penn. Mutual Life Ins. Co., Peoples Dispatch, Peoples Line, Phalons, Phelps. Nickel, cop., br., and w. m. 12 to 24. 25 pieces

1465 Picard, Pinanet, Pizzini, Prudens. Cop. (1), brass (1), and w. m.; proof. 16. 18 pieces

1466 Phinn & Jamison (pierced), Pickin Phinn & Co., Pingree, Prosser & Wellwood, Public Square. Cop. and brass. 12 to 18. 9 pieces

1467 **Q**UEST, J. W., Louisville. Ky. Brass. 16.

1468 **R**AINE, Charles J., Lynchburg, Va. Brass. 18.

1469 Randall & Co., Baltimore. From the same dies. *Silver.* 10.   2 pieces

1470 Randel, J., Jr. c. & D. CANAL 1825. Rev. Blank. Copper. 15.

1471 Richardson, W. & Co., Philadelphia and New York. Two duplicates in the lot. Copper (1) and brass. 15 and 17.   10 pieces

1472 Risley & McCollum's Hippodrome. Rev. " Troisieme." Brass. 20.

1473 Robinson, L., Chittenango, N. Y. Tin. 17.

1474 Ruelius. G. J., Philadelphia. Cop. & br. 13.   2 pieces

1475 R. M. & Co. (25c.), Rahm, Randall, Richards, Richardson, Rickey, Riker, Robbins, Royce & Hand, Robinson, Robinson Jones & Co., Root's, Root & Co., Ross, Ruggles. Nic., cop., br. and w. m. 10 to 24. 31 pieces

1476 Reed, Rice, Rowell. Cop. (2) and w. m. ; proof. 16.   14 pieces

1477 **S**AFFORD, N., Temperance House, Albany Copper. 20.

1478 Sage, A. B. & Co. New York. Cop., br., and w. m. 10 to 19.   10 pieces

1479 Sampson, H. G., New York. Rev. "Declaration of Independence." *Silver :* proof. 26.

1480 The same. Cop. and tin : proof. 26.   2 pieces

1481 Sharpless Brothers. Philadelphia. *Silver,* nickel, and brass. 18.   3 pieces

1482 Sheerer, J. W. & Co. Rev. "Drayage, 25 cents." Brass. 19.

1483 S. McD. & Co. Rev. "25 cents." Brass. 17.

1484 Smith, A. C., Dover, N H. 1837. Copper. 17.

1485 Smith, C. A. M., Windsor, N. Y. Copper. 17.

1486 Smith's Clock Establishment. 1837. 5 varieties. Cop. and brass. 18.   8 pieces

1487 Smith & Brothers, Philadelphia. Brass. 16.

1488 Spering, Mixsell and Innes, Philadelphia. Brass. 17.

1489 Squire & Merritt, New York. Copper. 17.

1490 Steamer Lancaster, No. 4. Rev. "The wealth of the South," " No submission to the North." etc. Cop. and brass. 13.   11 pieces

1491 Stevenson, Wm., Pittsburgh, Pa. Rev. Blank. Brass. 19.

1492 St. Louis Post Office. Rev. Name engraved. Cop. 17.

1493 Stockman & Co., Memphis. Rev. "Wealth of the South," "No submission to the North," etc. Copper and brass. 13. 12 pieces

1494 Stokes, Granville, Philadelphia. Brass. 19.

1495 Stokes, G. "Fine clothing, 607 Chestnut st., Phila." Rev. A piece of Atlantic cable inserted in the planchet. Grooved edge ; tin. Size 14 and quarter inch thick.

1496 Sylvester, J. A. & Co., Selma, Ala. Brass ; proof. 18.

1497 Sweeny's Hotel. Different values stamped on rev. German silver. 20. 8 pieces

1498 The same. Rev. "Smithsonian," "A. D. Thompson," etc. Cop. and brass. 16. 5 pieces

1499 Sanford, Sampsons, Schenck, Schmidt, Seagel, Scovill, Scoville Manufacturing Company, &c., Daguerreotype materials, Sines & Co., Simpson, Sise & Co., Sleeper & Fenner, Smith Murphy & Co., Smith & Hartman, Smith, Jas. S. & Co., Smithsonian House, Squire & Sons. Nickel, cop., br., and w. m. 14 to 22. 30 pieces

1500 Squire, Louis L. & Sons, New York. Silver. 18.

1501 Server, J W. Scott & Co., C. B. Scott & Co., Saussur, Daugler & Co. One pierced. W. m. ; proof. 15. 17 pieces

1502 Sperry (calendar for 1855), Starr, Starbuck & Son, Starwood & Co., Stanton (10 cents), Steppacher, Stephenson, Stockwell, Stone & Murray's Circus, Stoner & Shrover, Straight's Enthanting Shoe, Strasbinger and Nunn. Stamps, Suit "Salt River Bourbon," plain and milled edges. Sweet. Nickel, copper, brass, and white metal. 12 to 24, one piece pierced. 25 pieces

1503 Swoopes, Stilz & Son. W. m. ; proof. 16. 8 pieces

1504 **T**ALBOT, Allum & Lee, New York. 1794. Copper ; milled. 13. 2 pieces

1505 Taylor Co., N. & G., Philadelphia. Copper, brass, and w. m. 16 and 24. 5 pieces

1506 Thomas, W. A., Buffalo. Copper. 20 and 24. 3 pieces

1507 Taylor, Taylor & Raymond, Thompson, Throckmorton, T. P. D., Transfer Ticket, Troy, Tuttle, Tyler, Tyson & Co. Nickel, cop., brass, and w. m. two pierced. 14 to 18. 14 pieces

1508 Traphagen, Hunter & Co., Trenton. White m., one pierced. 16. 10 pieces

1509 **U**PMEYER. H., Milwaukee.   Nickel and copper.
     12.   2 pieces

2 1510 **V** AN Nostrand & Dwight. New York. 17.
2 1511 Valentine's Varnish, Van Cott. Vine Street Line,
     Voderbug. Cop. and brass. 5 to 23.   6 pieces
/ 1512 Vallee, Weidener. Whitman & Sons, Dr. Williams. W.
     m., proof. 16.   15 pieces

4 1513 **W**ALTON & Co. New Orleans. Brass. 20.
5 1514 Warner, C. K., Philadelphia. Bust of Washington, 15
     different reverses. Nickel, cop., brass and w. m. 17.
     37 pieces.
2 1515 The same. Cop., brass and w. m. 16.   3 pcs
3 1516 Walker, Walsh, Wanamaker & Brown, Ware, Water-
     bury Brass Co. (varieties. pierced), Waters & Sons,
     Wedding and Visiting Cards, Weighell & Sons (20
     cents), West, Whitney Glass Works, Whitney, Wolfe
     (Washington & George IV., do. and Jackson, the lat-
     ter pierced), cop., br. and white metal. 12 to 18. 25 pcs
** 1517 Wolff, James E., Petersburg, Va. *Silver.* 15.
c 1518 Wood's Minstrels, New York. *Silver.* 15.
3 1519 Woodgate & Co., New York. Six different reverses.
     Copper, brass, and w. m. 17.   13 pieces
4 1520 Wilbur, Col. Wood's Museum, Wilkins, Willard, Wise,
     Wolfe, Wolff, Woodworth, Woodcock. Copper, br.
     and w. m. 15 to 21.   17 pieces

2 9 1521 **Y**ALE, C. Jr. & Co., New Orleans. Brass. 17.
(1522 Yates & Co., A. O. Yates. Copper, brass and w. m.
     14 to 17.   3 pieces
/ 1523 **Z**AHN, S. H., Lancaster, Pa. Brass and white metal.
     12.   2 pieces
/ 1524 Miscellaneous. Several rare. Brass, etc., one pierced.
                                                 9 pieces
- 1525 Brass shells, etc., printed ads. on rev. Dollars, 1796,
     1867, $20 gold, etc. A few dupl. Very fine lot. 25 ps
: 1526 Rubber cards. Many varieties.   28 pieces

WAR TOKENS OR COPPERHEADS.

1527 Collection of War tokens, or Copperheads, alphabeti-
     cally arranged, and containing few if any duplicates,
     except in different metals. Nearly all copper; in
     condition generally uncirc. Aver. size 12. 1974 pcs

1528 Unassorted. Nearly all uncirculated. 524 pieces

1529 Large copperheads. A few duplicates. Copper and
brass (2). Uncirculated; a very rare lot. Average
size 15. 127 pieces

1530 P. Brimelow, Druggist, New York, and a few other
large copperheads. Nickel, copper, brass. Nearly
all size 15. 37 pieces

1531 The same. Varieties. *Silver*; nearly pr. 15. 3 pcs.

1532 Bust of Washington. Varieties. *Silver*, dime size;
uncirculated and rare. 4 pieces

1533 Bust of Lincoln. Varieties. *Silver*; unc. or pr. 6 pcs

1534 Bust of Burnside. "Rhode Island first in the field."
1864. Rev. Phillips' card, Providence, R. I. *Silver*;
uncirculated.

1535 Bust of Franklin. Rev. Bruas Bros., N.Y. *Silver*; unc.

1536 Head of Liberty, etc. Varieties, several struck over
dimes. *Silver*; uncirculated. 9 pieces

1537 Miscellaneous. *Silver*; several struck over dimes. Another rare lot; uncirculated. 15 pieces

AMERICAN MEDALS

PRESIDENTIAL AND POLITICAL.

1538 John Adams. Bust to right. Rev. Residence. Red
bronze; proof. 22.

1539 Thomas Jefferson. Bust to left. Rev. Peace and friendship. Bronze; very fine. 47.

1540 Bust to left. Rev. Minerva near a rock inscribed constitution, etc. to commemorate july 4, 1776.
Tin; fair only; rare. 28.

1541 Bust to right. Rev. Residence. Cop.; proof. 22.

1542 Bust to right, by *Bolen*. Rev. equal and exact
justice, etc. Cop., br. and w. m.; proof. 16. 3 pcs

1543 James Madison. Bust to right. Rev. Eagle with
implements of agriculture in his talons and a wreath.
industry brings plenty, etc. Tin; very thick
planchet and fine. 40.

1544 Bust to right. Rev. Residence. Cop.; nearly proof. 22.

1545 James Monroe. Bust to right, by *Furst*. Rev.
peace and friendship. Bronze; extremely fine.
48.

1546 Bust to right by *Furst.* Rev. PEACE AND FRIENDSHIP. Bronze; extremely fine. 40.

1547 Similar. Bronze : extremely fine. 34.

1548 Bust to right. Rev. Residence. Cop.: proof. 22.

1549 John Quincy Adams. Bust to right. Rev. PEACE AND FRIENDSHIP. Bronze; very fine. 39.

1550 Bust to right. Rev. Residence. Cop., proof. 22.

1551 Andrew Jackson. Bust to right by Furst. Rev. PEACE AND FRIENDSHIP. Red bronze : proof. 40.

1552 Large bust nearly facing. Rev. Star, UNITED STATES OF AMERICA. Tin ; very good. 28.

1553 The same obverse. Rev. Blank ; poor. 28.

1554 Bust to right. Rev. Residence. Copper : proof. 22.

1555 Bust to right. OLD HICKORY TOOK THE RESPONSIBILITY. Rev. Inscription in 14 lines. Copper and w. metal ; proof. 21.   2 pieces

1556 Jackson on horseback, to left. Rev. Bust of Harrison. *Silver ;* proof. 18.

1557 Bust to right, by *Bolen.* Rev. THE STERN OLD SOLDIER, etc. Cop., br., and w. m. : proof. 16.   3 pieces

1558 Bust to left. Rev. INAUG. ; SECOND TERM, etc. *Silver ;* proof. 12.

1559 Miscellaneous. No duplicates. Fair to fine. 2 pierced. Cop. (4), brass (5), w. m. (1). A scarce lot. 12 to 18.
                                                       9 pieces

1560 Martin Van Buren. Bust to right, by *Furst.* Rev. PEACE AND FRIENDSHIP. Bronze; perfect. 40.

1561 Similar medal. Bronze : perfect. 32.

1562 Bust to right. Rev. Residence. Copper : proof. 22.

1563 Bust to left. THE FEARLESS DEMOCRAT. Rev. Inscription in 12 lines. Copper : proof. 22.

1564 Miscellaneous. Brass : pierced. 14 to 18.   3 pieces

1565 William H. Harrison. Large bust nearly facing. Rev. Blank. Tin : fine. 28.

1566 Bust to left by *Mitchell, Boston.* Rev. HARRISON JUBILEE, BUNKER HILL, SEPT. 10, 1840. Bronze; very fine and rare. 27.

1567 Bust in toga to right. Rev. Eagle in circle of stars. W. m. : proof. 24.

1568 Bust to right. HONOR WHERE HONOR'S DUE, etc. Rev. Bunker Hill Monument. Yellow bronze : very fine. 24.

1569 The same obv. Rev. Blank. **Nickel** : very fine. 24.

1570 Bust to left. Rev. Log cabin, flags to right and left.
    Tin; pierced. Good and fine. 23. 2 pieces

1571 Bust to right. Rev. Residence. Cop.; proof. 22.

1572 Bust to left. Rev. Log cabin. THE PEOPLE'S CHOICE.
    Copper; proof. 22.

1573 Log cabin as in last No. HE IS A FREEMAN, etc. Tin;
    very fine. 22.

1574 Log cabin as before. Rev. Blank. Tin; silvered. V. f.

1575 Bust to right. Rev. BATTLE OF THAMES, etc. Silvered;
    pierced. Poor. 19.

1576 The same. Copper; pierced. Fair. 19.

1577 Bust to left in semi-circle of stars. Rev. Bust of Henry
    Clay. *Silver*; proof. 18.

1578 Miscellaneous. 7 pierced; nearly all fine and scarce.
    No dupl. Cop. and brass. 14 to 18. 40 pieces

1579 John Tyler. Bust to left. Rev. PEACE AND FRIEND-
    SHIP. Bronze; perfect. 48.

1580 Peace medal. Another; bronze; perfect. 40.

1581 Bust to right. Rev. Residence. Cop.; proof. 22.

1582 James K. Polk. Bust to left. Rev. PEACE AND FRIEND-
    SHIP. Bronze; perfect. 40.

1583 Busts of Polk and Dallas facing. Rev. SUCCESS WILL
    CROWN OUR EFFORTS. Tin; pierced. Fine. 28.

1584 Bust to left. Rev. Bust of Dallas. W. m.; pierced.
    Good. 26.

1585 Bust to right. Rev. Residence. Cop.; proof. 22.

1586 Henry Clay. Bust to left. Rev. Hand laid on a rock
    inscribed CONSTITUTION. THE ELOQUENT DEFENDER
    OF NATIONAL RIGHTS AND NATIONAL INDEPENDENCE.
    Bronze; rare and perfect. 48.

1587 Bust to left. Rev. Angel writing on monument. White
    metal; proof. 27.

1588 Bust to left, by *Lovett*. Rev. THE WEALTH OF A
    NATION, etc. Tin; thick and fine. 26.

1589 Miscellaneous. W. m.; 4 pierced. 29 to 36. 8 pieces

1590 Bust to left in heavy wreath of oak. Rev. NOMINATED
    BY THE BALTIMORE CONVENTION, etc. Brass;
    fine. 28.

1591 Bust to right. Rev. THE ELOQUENT ADVOCATE, etc.
    Silver; proof. 18.

1592 Same obv. Rev. Jackson on horseback, and duplicate
    of last. Cop. and br.; proof. 18. 3 pieces.

1593 Bust to left. HENRY CLAY ELECTED PRESIDENT, etc. *one of the lying tokens.* Brass; pierced. Fine, but spotted on rev. Scarce. 16.

1594 Miscellaneous. No duplicates. Cop. and br. ; 4 pierced. 14 to 17.   6 pieces

1595 Zacharv Taylor. Bust to left. Rev. PEACE AND FRIENDSHIP. Bronze ; perfect. 48.

1596 Similar medal. Bronze ; perfect. 40.

1597 Bust to right. Rev. Inscription in 10 lines. Bronze ; perfect. 36.

1598 Bust to left. Rev. Trophy with tablet inscribed A LITTLE MORE GRAPE CAPTAIN BRAGG, etc. Tin ; fair, pierced. 26.

1599 Bust to right. Rev. Residence. Cop.; proof. 22.

1600 Miscellaneous. Cop, br. and w. m.; the latter pierced. Fine. 18 and 20.   3 pieces

1601 Millard Fillmore. Bust to right by *Ellis.* Rev. Western pioneer and Indian facing. Bronze ; perfect. 40.

1602 Bust to right by *Odling.* Rev. THE UNION, and NO NORTH, NO SOUTH, etc. W. m. Fine. 24.   2 pcs

1603 Bust to right. Rev. Residence. Copper; proof. 22.

1604 Bust to right. Rev. BE VIGILANT, etc. W. m.; pr. 22.

1605 Bust to right. Rev. UNITED STATES OF AMERICA. Brass ; var., one pierced.   2 pieces

1606 Franklin Pierce. Bust to left. Rev. Trophy. W. m. ; proof. 26.

1607 Bust to right. Rev. Residence. Cop.; proof. 22.

1608 Miscellaneous. Brass; one pierced. Fine. 16 and 17.   2 pieces

1609 Winfield Scott. Bust to left in wreath of oak. Rev. NOMINATED, etc., 1852. Bronze ; very fine. 22.

1610 Miscellaneous. Brass and w. m., one pierced; good. 16 to 19.   4 pieces

1611 James Buchanan. Bust to right by *Ellis.* Rev. View of a settlement near the sea-shore ; broad border with Indian scalping an enemy, etc. Bronze ; perfect. 48.

1612 Bust to right by *Paquet.* Rev. Esculapius protecting female from death. Awarded Dr. Rose for kindness, etc. Bronze : perfect. 48.

1613 Same obv. Rev. IN COMMEMORATION OF THE FIRST EMBASSY FROM JAPAN TO THE UNITED STATES, 1860. Bronze ; perfect. 48.

1614 Bust nearly facing. Rev. Radiant eagle, names of States between the rays. THE UNION MUST AND SHALL BE PRESERVED. Tin; fine. 38.

1615 Bust to right. Rev. Residence. Copper, proof. 22.

1616 Bust to left. Rev. BORN NOV. 13 1791, etc. Copper, proof. 20.

1617 Miscellaneous. Br. and w. m., two pierced. 18 to 22. 4 ps.

1618 John C. Fremont. Large head to left. Rev. PEOPLE'S CHOICE 1856, etc. W m.; fine. 38.

1619 Bust to right. Rev. Surveying party. Tin, uncir. 27.

1620 Bust nearly facing. FREE SPEECH, etc. Rev. Soldiers raising U. S. flag on mountain peak. Tin; silvered. Uncirculated. 22.

1621 Bust to right. Rev. FREE SOIL. etc., in wreath. Bronze ; uncirculated. 21.

1622 Miscellaneous. Copper, br. and w. m., three pierced. 14 to 24. 6 pieces

1623 Stephen A. Douglass. Bust nearly facing. Rev. DEMO-CRATIC CANDIDATE, etc., in heavy wreath of oak. Copper, proof. 24.

1624 Miscellaneous. Brass and w. m.; one pierced. Fine. 20 to 24. 3 pieces

1625 Bust nearly facing. Rev. THE CHAMPION, etc. Nickel, copper, brass, and w. m.; pierced. 18. 4 pieces

1626 Miscellaneous. Cop., br., w. m., and rubber (1). 16 and 17. Very fine. 8 pieces

1627 Bust to left. Rev. THE WEALTH OF THE SOUTH and President's House. Cop., brass and w. m.; fine, one pierced. 14. 4 pieces

1628 Bust nearly facing. Rev. INTERVENTION IS DISUNION, 1860. Different metals; pierced. 12. 4 pieces

1629 Bust nearly facing. LITTLE GIANT. Rev. THE DECLAR-ATION OF INDEPENDENCE WAS ADOPTED JULY 4, 1776. Also same as last. Var. metals; proof. 12. 6 pcs

1630 John Bell. Bust to left. Rev. Eagle. W. m.; pr. 24.

1631 Miscellaneous. Copper, br., and w. m.; all very fine. 16 to 20. 8 pieces

1632 Wm. H. Seward. Varieties. Brass; fine. 17. 2 pieces

1633 Abraham Lincoln. Bust to right, by Nigel. Rev. IN MEMORY OF THE LIFE ACTS AND DEATH OF ABRAHAM LINCOLN BORN FEBRUARY 12 1809 DIED APRIL 14 1865. Issued by the Amer. Numismatic and Archæ-ological Society of New York. Bronze; perfect impression. A rare and most beautiful medal. 52.

1634 Large bust to left. DEDIE PAR LA DEMOCRATIE FRAN-
CAISE A LINCOLN, etc. Rev. Angel placing a crown
on a monument around which freedmen are gathered.
LINCOLN HONNETE HOMME ABOLIT L'ESCLAVAGE
RETABLIT L'UNION, etc. A superb medal gotten up
in France by penny subscription, struck in Switzerland. Bronze ; proof. 52.

1635 Bust to right by *Ellis*, 1862. Rev. Western scene ;
Indian scalping an enemy on border. Bronze ; perfect. 40.

1636 Large bust to right by *Bovy*. Rev. ABOLITION OF SLA-
VERY PROCLAIMED SEPTEMBER 22D 1862. WITH
MALICE TOWARD NONE, etc. Bronze ; proof. 38.

1637 Bust to right by *Key*. Rev. Broken column. HE IS IN
GLORY AND THE NATION IN TEARS. Yellow bronze.
Fine, and a rare medal. 32.

1638 The same. White metal ; proof. 32.

1639 Bust to right by *Barber*. Rev. EMANCIPATION PRO-
CLAIMED JAN. 1 1863. U. S. Mint series. Bronze ;
perfect. 28.

1640 Bust to left. Rev. THE RAILSPLITTER OF 1830 W. m.
Fine. 26.

1641 Busts facing of Lincoln and Johnson. Rev. Inscription.
White metal ; proof. 26.

1642 Bust to right. Rev. CENTENNIAL OF AMERICAN INDE-
PENDENCE, etc. White metal ; proof. 25.

1643 Same obv. Rev. THOU ART THE MAN, PRESIDENT 1861.
White metal ; proof. 25.

1644 Old head to right. Rev. PROGRESS 1830. Wh. metal ;
fine. 24.

1645 Duplicates of five last numbers. Same condition. 5 pcs

1646 Bust to right. Rev. Rails crossed. THE PEOPLES
CHOICE 1860, etc. Copper : silvered. Extremely
fine. 24.

1647 Bust to right. Rev Eagle. Type metal ; pierced. Uncirculated. 24.

1648 Bust to left, surrounded by stars. Rev. Crossed rails
with roosting fowls. THE GREAT RAILSPITTER OF
THE WEST MUST, etc. Copper : proof 22.

1649 Bust to left. Rev. THE RIGHT MAN, etc., in wreath,
1861. Copper, proof. 21.

1650 Bust to right. HONEST OLD ABE. Rev. UNION CAN-
DIDATE, etc. 1864. W. m. ; proof. 21.

1651 Duplicates of three last Nos. W. m. ; 1 pierced. 3 pieces

1652 Bust to left, same as in 1648. Rev. Bust to right.
ABRAHAM LINCOLN SIXTEENTH PRESIDENT OF THE
U. S. Tin. fine. 22.

1653 Bust to right. Rev. LET LIBERTY BE NATIONAL AND
SLAVERY SECTIONAL. Cop., br. and w. m.; proof.
20. 3 pieces

1654 Bust to right. Rev. Fasces, in type UNITED, etc.
W. m.; proof. 20.

1655 Same obv. Rev. OUR NEXT PRESIDENT. W. m.; proof. 20.

1656 Bust to right. Rev. NO MORE SLAVE TERRITORY, 1860.
Cop.; proof. 19.

1657 Bust to right. Rev. THE WAR THAT CAM SPLET BALD,
etc. Brass; very fine, pierced. 19.

1658 Miscellaneous; includes dupl. of last Rev. Copper and
w. m., 3 pierced. 19. 7 pieces

1659 Bust to right. Rev. r. s. in trophy. Brass; unc. 19.

1660 Bust to left. 8 stars and 1864 below. Rev. Bust of
McClellan to right. White metal; proof. 19.

1661 Bust to right, by F. B. Smith. WAR OF 1861, etc.
Brass; proof. 18.

1662 Bust to right. Rev. Eagle, with union, etc. Brass;
proof. 18.

1663 Bust to right. Rev. FREE HOMES FOR FARMERS, in
small circle, etc. Cop., br. and w. m. 17. 3 pieces

1664 The same obverse. Rev. Legend in circle of stars.
Brass; proof. 17.

1665 Long bust to right. Rev. THE RAILSPLITTER OF THE
WEST. Cop., br., etc.; proof. 17. 4 pieces

1666 Bust to left, the field dotted with stars. Rev. THE
CONSTITUTION AND THE UNION, etc. Cop., br. and
w. m.; proof. 17. 2 pcs.

1667 Urn under weeping willow tree. A NATION THE ARREST
CLAIM, THE DEAD A TEAR. Rev. ABM. LINCOLN
DIED APRIL 15 1865 BY THE HANDS OF A BASE AS-
SASSIN. W. m.; uninscribed and perf. 17.

1668 Bust to right. Rev. Bust of U. S. Grant. Silver;
proof. 16.

1669 Bust to right. Rev. WITH MALICE TOWARD NONE WITH
CHARITY TO ALL. Bronze, copper, br. and w. m.
Proof. 16. 4 pieces

1670 Bust to right. 1860. Rev. OUR READER, etc. Bronze
and brass; proof. 16. 2 pieces

1671 Bust to right. Rev. SLAVERY NATIONAL, SLAVERY
SECTIONAL. Cop., br. and w. m. Proof. 16. 3 pcs.

1672 Bust to right, 25 (cents) below. IN GOD WE TRUST. Rev. Eagle with arrows and olive branch. UNITED STATES OF AMERICA, etc. 1864. Copper, br. and w. m. 16. 3 pieces

1673 Miscellaneous. A few dupl. of last Nos. Copper, br. and w. m.; one rubber. Proof. 14 to 18. 6 pieces

1674 Bust to right. 1864. Rev. Trophy. OUR COUNTRY AND OUR FLAG, etc. Copper and br., proof. 14. 2 pieces

1675 Same obv. Rev. BORN FEB 12 1809, ASSASSINATED APRIL 14TH 1865. Copper and w. m.; proof. 14. 2 pieces

1676 Bust facing. FREE LAND, FREE SPEECH, etc. Rev. Eagle over eight stars. Brass; fine and rare. 14.

1677 Bust to right by *Key*. PRESIDENT 1861-1865 Rev. SHALL BE THEN, THENCEFORWARD AND FOREVER FREE *Silver ;* very fine and scarce.

1678 Bust to left. Rev. President's House, star in wreath, and blank. Copper, br. and w. m. Very fine. 14. 5 pcs

1679 Large head to right. ABRAHAM LINCOLN. Brass, silvered, the rev. blank. Rare. 14.

1680 Oval medalet with loop. Large bust to left. Rev. MARTYR TO LIBERTY, etc. Copper, gilt. 13 x 14.

1681 The same. Bronze, proof.

1682 Bust to right. 1864. Rev. Trophy (varieties) and bust of Grant. Copper, br. and w. m. Two pierced; proof. 12. 6 pieces

1683 Naked bust to right, without legend. Rev. Head of Grant, trophy, Centennial bell. Bronze and w. m., proof. 12. 3 pieces

1684 Bust to right. NATUS FEB 12 1809. Rev. WIDE AWAKES, etc. Copper and w. m., proof. 12. 2 pcs

1685 Same obv. Rev. ABRA-HAM LIN-COLN THE HANNIBAL OF AMERICA. Nickel and w. m. 12. 2 pieces

1686 Bust to right. 1864; 35 stars near border. Rev. LINCOLN AND UNION. Brass; proof. 12.

1687 1864 Copperheads. Different reverses : copper and brass, proof. 3 pieces

1688 Bust to left. LINCOLN AND LIBERTY. Rev. GOOD FOR ANOTHER HEAT. Brass ; fine, pierced. 12.

1689 Head to right. FOR PRESIDENT, etc. Rev. Head of Johnson. Copper. 12. 2 pieces

1690 Head to left. 1864. Thirteen stars near border. Rev. FREEDOM JUSTICE TRUTH 1865. Brass; pierced. 8.

1691 John C. Breckinridge. Bust to left. Rev. Eagle and thirteen stars. White metal: fine. 24.

1692 Head to left. 1860. Rev. OUR COUNTRY AND OUR RIGHTS in wreath of oak and laurel. Copper: uncirculated and rare. 15.

1693 Bust to left. JOHN C. BRECKINRIDGE FOR PRESIDENT. Rev. PRESIDENTS HOUSE. Copper and br.; uncirculated. 14.   2 pieces

1694 Geo. B. McClellan. Head to left, by Lovett, Phila. COMMANDER ARMY OF THE POTOMAC. Rev. Names of battles. Tin; very fine and rare. 30.

1695 Bust to left. Rev. SEC QUERRRE SEC SPERNERE HONOREM in wreath: shields, drum, etc., below. Bronze: very fine. 22.

1696 Bust to left. GEO. B. MCCLELLAN FOR PRESIDENT. 1864. Rev. Shield on trophy. Brass: fine and scarce. 19.

1697 Same obv. Rev. Eagle on a trophy. Brass: fair, pierced. 19.

1698 Bust to left between branches of oak and laurel crossed. Rev. Trophy, with shield inscribed THE PEOPLES CHOICE, etc. Copper and br.: very fine. 20. 2 pcs

1699 Bust to left, a star below. Rev. FIRST IN THE HEART OF HIS SOLDIERS around a wreath. Copper: very fine, pierced. 20.

1700 Bust to left, WAR OF 1861 below. Rev. Blank. Brass; very fine, pierced. 19.

1701 Large bust to left, by Merriam. BORN DEC 3 1826. Rev. Trophy. W. m. silvered and proof. 19.

1702 Bust to right. 1864. Rev. Same as rev. of 1698. Nickel and brass; fine. 20.   2 pieces

1703 Miscellaneous. Two duplicates of preceding lots, two pierced. W. m.: fine to proof. 17 to 22. 8 pieces

1704 Bust to left. Rev. Monitor. Bronze, copper and w. m.: proof. 18.   3 pieces

1705 Miscellaneous. Copper and brass, 2 pierced: fine. 10 to 14.   5 pieces

1706 Andrew Johnson. Bust to right, by Zeitler. 1867. Rev. WITH COURAGE AND FIDELITY, etc. in wreath of oak and laurel. Bronze; perfect. 45.

1707 Bust to left. PRESIDENT U. S. Rev. NATIONAL UNION CONVENTION, etc. Bronze and w. m. proof. 29. 2 pcs

1708 Andrew Johnson " 17 President." Varieties. W. m. 11 and 12.   2 pcs

◡ 1709 Horatio Seymour. 1868. Bust facing.· Rev. WHITE
MEN TO GOVERN. White metal ; fine. 20.

◡ 1710 Bust to right. Rev. DEMOCRATIC CANDIDATE, etc. Copper, br., and white metal : proof. 18.　　　3 pieces

2 1711 Bust to right. Rev. FOR PRESIDENT, etc., 1868. Cop.
and w. m.; proof. 12.　　　2 pieces

), ∠ ◡ ⁻ 1712 U. S. Grant. Military bust, nearly facing. GENERAL
U. S. GRANT. *Hugues Bovy fecit Geneve (Suisse).*
Rev. PATIENT OF TOIL, SERENE, etc., in four lines;
near the border, I INTEND TO FIGHT IT OUT, etc. A
superb and extremely rare medal. *Silver,* proof. 38.

1713 Military bust to left. GENERAL U. S. GRANT. 1868.
Hugues Bovy fecit Geneve (Suisse). Rev. Same as rev.
of last No. *Silver ;* proof. A very beautiful and rare
medal. 38.

1714 The same. Bronze ; proof. 38.

1715 Bust to right by *Key.* Rev. INAUGURATED PRESIDENT,
etc., 1869, in wreath ; yellow bronze ; fine. 32.

1716 Naked bust to right. PRESIDENCY OF U. S. GRANT.
In exergue, THE OCEANS UNITED, etc. Rev. Rocky
Mountain scenery ; a train of cars passing. EVERY
MOUNTAIN SHALL BE MADE LOW, on scroll above.
Silver proof medal by *Barber.* 28.

◡ 1 1717 Bust, similar to last. U. S. GRANT PRESIDENT UNITED
STATES. Rev. Ornamental design with broad tablet
inscribed LIBERTY THE TRUE FOUNDATION . . . LET
US HAVE PEACE, etc. Bronze; proof. 28.

0 1718 Bust to right. LIEUT. GEN. U. S. GRANT and 13 stars :
wreath of laurel near border. Rev. Trophy and
shield. W. m.: proof. 25.

∟ 0 1719 Busts jugata to left, 1872. THE NATICK COBBLER THE
GALENA TANNER. Rev. GRANT AND WILSON, THERE'S
NOTHING LIKE LEATHER. Genuine *leather* medal, in
finest possible condition. Rare. 24.

◡ 1720 Busts jugata to right, by *Sigel.* U. S. GRANT, S. COLFAX.
Rev. FOR PRESIDENT, etc. 1869–1873. White metal,
very fine. 24.

1 1721 Military bust to left. REPUBLICAN CANDIDATE, etc.
Rev. I INTEND TO FIGHT IT OUT, etc. Copper, br.
and white metal ; proof. 20.　　　3 pieces

1722 Military bust to right. GENERAL U. S. GRANT. Rev.
Bust of Colfax, 1868, etc. W. m., proof. 20.

1723 Military bust to right. LIEU. GEN. U. S. GRANT. Rev.
CAPTURE OF RICHMOND, APRIL 3RD, 1865. Copper,
proof, very scarce. 19.

1724 Same obverse. Rev. Star-like ornament. Copper: nearly proof. 19.

1725 Bust to right. Rev. GRANT, etc. Brass shell: fine. 22.

1726 Military bust to left, by *Lovibus*, GRANT & COLFAX, etc., 1868. Rev. MATCH EM: THE HOPE OF THE NATION in wreath. W. m.; very fine. 20. 2 pcs

1727 Bust to right. Rev. RECEPTION OF EX-PRESIDENT U. S. GRANT AT PHILADELPHIA DEC. 16, 1879. W. m.; proof. 18.

1728 Military bust to left, by *Key*, four stars below. Rev. SURRENDER OF GENERAL LEE, etc., 1865. Copper and w. m.; proof. 18. 2 pieces

1729 Same obverse. Rev. IN HONOR OF THE 15TH AMENDMENT, etc., 1870. W. m.; proof. 18.

1730 Military bust to left, by *Key*, four stars, close together, below. Rev. REPUBLICAN CANDIDATE, etc. Brass and w. m.; proof. 17. 2 pieces

1731 Large bust in uniform to left. Rev. SURRENDER OF GEN. LEE, etc. W. m.; proof. 18.

1732 Bust nearly facing. Rev. I INTEND, etc. Copper and br. silv. Proof. 18. 2 pieces

1733 Duplicates of last No. Brass and silvered. Pierced. 3 pieces

1734 Busts jugate of Grant and Colfax. 1868. Rev. LET US HAVE PEACE, in wreath. Copper, brass and w. m.; proof. 18. 3 pieces

1735 Bust to left. ULYSSES S. GRANT. Rev. STRUCK AND DISTRIBUTED IN THE MUNICIPAL PARADE etc., 1872. Copper gilt; proof.

1736 Duplicates of Nos. 1725, 26, 35. W. m.; two pierced. Also busts facing of Grant and Colfax; trial piece in lead and rubber card. 16 to 20. 6 pieces

1737 Bust to right, by *Balen*. Rev. OUR NEXT PRESIDENT, etc. Copper, br., and w. m. 16. 3 pieces

1738 Bust to right by *Key*. Rev. REPUBLICAN CANDIDATE, etc. 1872. Cop. and w. m.; proof. 16. 2 pcs

1739 Bust to right. VICKSBURG, JULY 4, 1862. Rev. THE UNION MUST AND SHALL BE PRESERVED, etc. Copper; proof. 15.

1740 Brass shells; silvered. Varieties in bust, etc. 15. 2 pieces

1741 Bust to right. PRES. 1869 TO '77 on label below. Rev. CIVIS LONDINENSIS JULY 13TH, 1877. A CIVIC GRANT FOR ALABAMA CLAIMS. Brass; proof. 14.

1742 Same as last, with the addition on rev. of *I. F. W. des.* Copper; proof. 14.

1743 Bust to right, 1868. Rev. PARMELEE, WEBSTER & CO., 155 JANE ST., N. Y. PURE ALUMINUM; "10" in centre. Copper and brass proof. 13. 2 pieces.

1744 Bust to left, 1868. Rev. Eagle and trophy. Cop. pr. 14.

1745 Large head to right. Rev. GENERAL U. S. GRANT in wreath. *Silver;* pr. 11.

1746 Varieties: one with head of Lincoln on rev. Copper and w. m.; proof. 11. 3 pieces

1747 HORACE GREELEY. Bust to right by *Key.* Rev. EDITOR AND FOUNDER OF THE N.Y. TRIBUNE, etc. Copper and brass proof. 16. 2 pieces

1748 Same obv. Rev. FOR PRESIDENT, etc. 1872. Copper and w. m.; proof. 16. 2 pieces

1749 "The Sage of Chappaqua," brass, pierced; Horace Greeley and B. Gratz Brown; brass shell silvered. 15. 2 pieces

1750 Rutherford B. Hayes, William A. Wheeler, Samuel J. Tilden. Varieties. Nickel, bronze and silv. brass. Two pierced; uncirculated. 20. 3 pieces

1751 Bust of Hayes to left. Rev. PRESIDENT, etc., 1876. Copper, brass, and w. m. (pierced); proof. 3 pieces

1752 Celluloid Campaign badges. Hayes, Wheeler, Tilden & Hendricks. All different colors. 16. 7 pieces

1753 James A. Garfield. Bust to left. THE NATION'S CHOICE, 1880. Rev. FROM THE TOW PATH TO THE WHITE HOUSE. Copper and gilt; proof. 18. 2 pcs

1754 The same. Varieties. Copper and white metal; proof, 2 pierced. 12 and 16. 3 pieces

1755 Bust of Garfield. Rev. Bust of Mrs. Garfield. Octagonal, pierced, with loop. *Gold.* 6.

1756 Winfield S Hancock. Rev. 2 A C on trefoil; crowing cock, " A combination." Brass and white metal; proof. 16 and 18. 3 pieces

ARMY AND NAVY.

The terms "perfect" and "very fine" when applied to medals mean of fine color, uncirculated.

1757 Horatio Gates. Bust by *Gatteaux.* For Saratoga, 1777. Bronze; perfect. 34.

1758 John Paul Jones. Bust by *Dupré.* For naval victory off coast of Scotland. 1799. Bronze; perfect. 36.

1759 Thomas Truxton. Bust to left, plain rim. For victory over French frigate La Vengeance. 1800. Bronze; perfect. 36.

1760 Edward R. McCall. Bust by *Furst*. For capture of Boxer, 1813. Bronze; perfect. 40.

1761 Lieut. W. Burroughs. A tomb and trophy of arms. Rev. View of engagement between the Enterprise and Boxer, during which he was killed. 1813. Bronze; perfect. 40.

1762 Brigadier Gen. James Miller. Bust by *Furst*. For battles of Chippewa and Niagara. 1814. Bronze; perfect. 40.

1763 Governor Isaac Shelby. Bust by *Furst*. For battle of the Thames. 1813. Bronze; perfect. 40.

1764 Lieut. Stephen Cassin. Bust by *Furst*. For victory on Lake Champlain. 1814. Bronze; perfect. 40.

1765 Captain Johnston Blakeley. Bust by *Furst*. For capture of British sloop Reindeer. 1814. Bronze; perfect. 40.

1766 Captain Robert Henley. Bust by *Furst*. For victory on Lake Champlain. 1814. Bronze; perfect. 40.

1767 Brig. Gen Eleazer W. Ripley. Bust by *Furst*. Rev. Fame hanging a shield inscribed CHIPPEWA, NIAGARA, ERIE to palm tree. 1814. Bronze; perfect. 40.

1768 Captain James Biddle. Bust by *Furst*. For capture of British ship Penguin. 1815. W. metal; perfect. 40.

1769 Major General Andrew Jackson. Bust by *Furst*. Rev. Figure of Victory inscribing the word ORLEANS on tablet, Peace behind her. 1815. Bronze; perfect. 42.

1770 Major General Winfield Scott. Bust by *Furst*. For battles of Chippewa and Niagara. 1814. Bronze; perfect. 40.

1771 The same. Bust to left by *Wright*. Rev. Views of six battles in Mexico in wreaths of oak and laurel; the American army before the city of Mexico in the centre. Bronze; perfect. 58.

1772 Major General Zachary Taylor. Bust to right by *Wright*. For battle of Buena Vista. 1847. Bronze; perfect. 56.

1773 The same. Bust to right. For Palo Alto and Resaca de la Palma. 1846. Bronze; perfect. 40.

1774 Major General Peter B. Porter. Bust by *Furst*. Victory with three flags, inscribed CHIPPEWA, NIAGARA, ERIE, before figure of Fame, who inscribes these names on a tablet. 1814. Bronze; perfect. 40.

1775 Bust of Gen. G. K. Warren, by *Key.* 1864. Rev. Army badge. COMMANDER OF THE 5TH CORPS, etc. Bronze; perfect. 24.

1776 Regimental badge of the 7th Regt. Inf. N. G., State of New York. Two oval shields, superimposed: the one on left with bust of Col. Clark: the other with laurel wreath. Rev. View of the new armory of the 7th Regiment, N. Y. 1879. *Silver;* proof, loop, very rare. 17 x 18.

1777 Regimental badge, with ribbon, 7th Inf. N. G. S. N. Y. PRO PATRIA ET GLORIA. Nov. 1879. *Silvered;* perfect. 26 x 28.

MASONIC MEDALS.

The references are to the Nos. in Marvin's Masonic Medals.

1778 Belgium. Eye in triangle over shield, OR : DE LIÉGE 5869. Rev. Two hands joined in triangle. Copper; very fine, pierced. 16. *M.* 41.

1779 France. L .˙. . DE LA PARFAITE UNION ET ST JEAN DU DESERT REUNIS. 1842. Brass; octagonal and fine. 15. *M.* 22.

1780 □ DES AMIS DE LA PAIX. Paris, 5789. Copper; very fine. 18. *M.* 28.

1781 Duplicates of Nos. 1778 and 1780. Very fine.   2 pcs

1782 L .˙. DES AMIS INCORRUPTIBLES, Paris 5785. Phoenix rising from pyre, and monogram in chain of love-knots. Copper; fine. 17. *M.* 73.

1783 LOGE DE ST EUGENE, Paris. 5805. Five pointed star in wreath, and radiant sun. Copper ; fine. 17. *M.* 75.

1784 ARDENTE AMITIE, Rouen. Triangle in radiant sun over altar and Masonic tools. Rev. Ivy clinging to a lifeless tree, etc. *Silver :* very good ; octagonal. 21. *M.* 99.

1785 COMMANDEURS DU MONT THABOR. 5807. Level in wreath and sun rising behind a mass of rocks. Copper : fine. 19.

1786 G.˙.O.˙.F.˙. Between two branches of myrtle an eagle on fasces. JUNCTI ROBORANTUR. Rev. Radiant sun with human face on triangle, a serpent around it. OMNIBUS UNUS. Copper; very fine. 18. *M.* 169, and ascribed to the year 1810.

1787 ☐ DU POINT PARFAIT. Paris, 5760. A man seated before a pyramid, behind which is a bush of acacia. Rev. Radiant sun over bee-hive and Masonic implement. Copper; fine. 18. *M.* 164.

1788 Duplicates of Nos. 1782, 1787. Copper; both fine. 2 pcs

1789 L.·. ECOSS.·.DES MILITAIRES RÉUNIS. Versailles. Ornamental shield with Masonic devices and three triangles interlinked. *Silver;* milled edge; very fine. 18. *M.* 237.

1790 L.·. ECOSSAISE DE JÉRUSALEM. Paris, 5817. Acacia bush, on the trunk of which are the letters R. J., on the left a triangle, on the right a gavel; POUR LES MACONS IL EST TOUJOURS FLEURI. Rev. Square and compasses over a radiant star, in the centre a trowel with letter G. Copper; fine. 19. Differs somewhat from the description given by Marvin (244), who had never seen this rare medal.

1791 L.·. D'ÉMETH RIT ÉCOSSAIS ANC ET ACCEPTE. Paris, 1822. Square, compasses, and triangle over radiant star, etc. Copper; fine. 17. *M.* 360.

1792 ☐ BONAPARTE. 5852. A bee. Rev. Square and comp. JETON DE PRÉSENCE. Brass; very fine. 16. *M.* 643.

1793 L'UNION FRATERNELLE. Troyes. 5850. Three towers within square and compasses. Rev. HUMANITÉ, JUSTICE, DÉVOUEMENT. Copper; very fine. 20. *M.* 665.

1794 CONSEIL DES G.·. GH.·. EL.·. K.·. S.·. DES 7 ÉCOSSAIS RÉUNIS. Paris. Double-headed eagle and Teutonic cross, etc. *Silver;* very fine. 15. *M.* 605.

1795 Germany. Bust of Zinnendorf, by *Hollenbach.* Rev. Interior of Gothic church, the names of Grand Masters in exergue, etc. *Silver;* a very fine and scarce medal. 36. *M.* 858.

1796 THREE GLOBES, 1840. Bust of Frédéric II. the Great, who introduced Freemasonry in Prussia, 1740. Rev. A curtain, etc. Bronze; very good. 32. *M.* 385.

1797 Netherlands. Radiant triangle enclosing Masonic maxims and inscription in ten lines. Struck by the *Loge Bien Aimée* of Amsterdam in 1885, on third centennial of date of a reputed Masonic document, known as the Charter of Cologne. Bronze. 32. *M.* 18.

1798 Military bust to left; FREDERIK PR.·. DES PAYS BAS. Rev. Radiant sun over Masonic implements and acacia branches. Struck on installation of the Grand Lodge of Southern Provinces of Holland, about 1818. *Silver;* very fine. 29. *M.* 205.

1799 United States. Masonic Temple, Boston. Dedication
    Medal, 1867. Tin, silvered ; fine. 20. *M.* 21.

1800 View of Old Masonic Hall, Broadway, N. Y. DEMOL-
    ISHED 1856. Sage's Masonic Medalets No. 1. Cop-
    per, proof. 20. *M.* 36.

1801 Masonic Temple, New York, Dedication Medal, 1875.
    Bronze ; uncir. 20. *M.* 37.

1802 Duplicates of Nos. 1800 and 1801. Same metal and
    condition.   2 pieces

1803 MARY COMMANDERY, 1876. Member's badge, with
    ribbon. W. m.; very fine. 23 by 29. *M.* 101.

1804 Bust of Washington to left ; 1776—1876, etc. Rev.
    Ground floor of a Masonic Temple. Brass ; proof.
    20. *M.* 268.

1805 Bust nearly facing, of Washington. Rev. Square,
    compasses, etc. *Harzfeld's series.* Brass, gilt ; proof.
    21. *M.* 275.

1806 New Masonic Temple, Phila. Dedication Medal, 1873.
    Copper ; very fine. 24. *M.* 284.

1807 Medalet, struck on the same occasion. *Silver, proof.*
    12. *M.* 285.

1808 Gercke's business token. Same obverse as last No.
    Copper, brass. W. m.; proof. 12. *M.* 286. 3 pcs

1809 OLIVE BRANCH □ No. 39, New York. Masonic em-
    blems, and view of the "Old Round House, Le Roy,
    N. Y." Copper ; uncirculated. 22. *M.* 288.

1810 LAKE CITY LODGE, NO. 27, FLA. Bronze ; uncir. ; new
    die, G. H. L. 17. *M.* 290.

1811 Bust of Kane, Arctic navigator over tablet representing
    Arctic scenery, etc. Rev. Ground floor of Masonic
    Temple. Bronze ; thick pl., perfect. 32. *M.* 291.

1812 Another. W. m. silvered. Very good. 32.

1813 HOPKINS LODGE 180, Texas. Square and compasses ;
    Rev. Inscription ; brass ; proof. 14. *M.* 301.

1814 Shield under eye, surrounded by 13 stars, HOL-
    LANDSCHE LOGE etc. Rev. FIRST MASTER JOHN
    MYER, etc. *Wood's Series.* Yellow bronze ; proof.
    20. *M.* 302.

1815 Old and new Masonic Temple, N. Y. A rare mule.
    Brass, proof. 20. *M.* 303.

1816 Within square and compasses, the bust of Washington
    to left, etc. Commemorates his visit to Solomon's
    Lodge, No. 1. Poughkeepsie, N. Y., December 27,
    1782. *Wood's Series. Silver ;* proof. 22. *M.* 307.

1817 The same. Brass; proof.

1818 Duplicates of Nos. 1800, 1801, 1809, and 1816. Copper and w. m.; proof or uncirculated. 4 pieces

1819 Square and compass, interlaced with the letter G. Rev. The Lord's prayer. *Silver*; struck at Philadelphia, 1876, on a cruciform planchet, with loop. Uncirculated. 10 x 12. *M.* 325.

1820 Within a wreath of wheat, grapes, and olive, a corner stone surmounted by three burning tapers. Rev. Trophy of regimental arms, flags, etc., surrounded by Masonic implements. This rare and beautiful medal was struck on the occasion of the laying of the corner stone of armory of Seventh Regiment, by the Grand Lodge of the State of New York, 1877. Yellow bronze; proof. 25. *M.* 711.

1821 The same. W. m.; proof. Rare.

1822 The Obelisk Medal. Bronze; proof. 22. *M.* 712.

1823 The same. Brass and w. m. proof. 2 pieces

1824 William Long, Phila. Masonic token. Copper; fine. 17. *M.* 723.

1825 Duplicates. Copper; fine. 2 pieces

1826 Token. Square and compasses. NO COMPROMISE WITH TRAITORS. Copper and w. m. Uncir. 12. 3 pieces

1827 Masonic copperheads. *M.* 726a and 728. All very fine. 4 pieces

1828 Engraved English medal. KING CH(apter). Various Masonic emblems on each side, beautifully engraved on an oval silver planchet. 29 x 40. VIRTVTE ET SILENTIO below. Scalloped border of 33 points, probably in allusion to the number of Masonic degrees. Metallic frame with loop; perfect.

The inscription, etc., shows this to have probably been made about the middle of the last century, and it is an excellent example of the early English Masonic Medals, which from their antiquity and rarity bring even better prices abroad than struck pieces.

1829 Engraved silver planchet, dollar size. Ground floor of Masonic Temple. Rev. B T W S S H K S in wreath. Fine.

1830 Temple of Honor medal. Triangle, bows and arrows, mystic cypher; pin, guard and ribbon attached. *Silver*; fine. Diameter of medal proper, 22.

1831 The same. Without pin, etc. *Silver*; fine. 22.

1832 Amulet or talisman. Stars, triangles etc., long cabalistic inscriptions in monkish Latin, etc. Probably medieval. Loop; copper, good condition. 33.

ENCASED POSTAGE STAMPS.

1833   Ayers' Sarsaparilla, 1c., 3c.,   2 pieces
1834   Ayers' Sarsaparilla, variety, 3c.
1835   Take Ayers' Pills, 1c., 3c.,   2 pieces
1836   The Currency to pass; varieties, 1c., 3c.,   2 pieces
1837   Drake's Plantation Bitters, 1c., 3c., 5c.,   3 pieces
1838   Gage, Bro., & Drake, 5c., 10c.,   2 pieces
1839   J. Gault, 3c., 5c., 10c., 12c.,   4 pieces
1840   Hunt & Nash, 10c.
1841   North American Life Ins., 1c.
1842   N. & G. Taylor Co., 1c.

CATALOGUES.

1843   1859, Dec. 19, 20, Jos. N. T. Levick; printed prices, interleaved. 4°.

1844   1860, May 21, 22, Edwd. Cogan; interleaved. 4°.

1845   1862, March 25, 26, Edwd. Cogan; printed prices, interleaved, clean. 4°.

1846   1862, Nov. 11–14, W. Elliot Woodward; printed prices, interleaved; only a few printed, clean. 4°.

1847   1863, Apr. 28, May 1, W. E. Woodward; printed prices, interleaved, only a few printed, clean. 4°.

1848   1863, Oct. 20, 21, J. Colburn; foreign coins, printed prices, interleaved, 10 printed, clean. 4°.

1849   1863, Oct. 20–24, J. Colburn; printed prices, interleaved, 10 printed, fine copy. 4°.

1850   1864, May 17–21, John F. McCoy; interleaved, heavy paper, 15 printed, fine copy.

1851   1864, May 15–21. Same; priced, and named complete, cover soiled.

1852   1870, Apr. 12, Birch, Phila.: clean. 4°.

1853   1870, Apr. 12. Same: priced, and named complete.

1854   1870, Oct. 4–7, Fewsmith; clean. 4°.

1855   1870, Oct. 4–7, Same: priced, and named, complete.

1856   1860, July 12, Bangs. Merwin, & Co.; priced.

1857   1864, Oct. 5, McGilvray & Co.; priced.

1858   1864, Jan. 20, Leavitt; soiled.

1859 1864, Jan. 13, 5th Ward Museum; clean.

1860 1866, May 24, Leonard & Co.; priced and named.

1861 1867, March 19, B. Scott, Jr., Phila.; priced, clean.

1862 1869, June 23, 24, M. L. Mackenzie : 5 plates.

1863 1874, June 16, etc., Leavitt : bric-a-brac, contains medals, clean.

1864 1874, March 18-21, Leavitt; antique, contains medals, clean.

1865 1874, Oct. 6-9, Leavitt ; 2 plates, clean.

1866 1874, Dec. 1, 2, Somerville; contains coins, clean.

1867 1874, Dec. 14, Bangs : contains medals.

1868 1874, Dec. 22, Leavitt : addenda, 100 printed, 1 sheet.

1869 1875, Apr. 8, Herts: furniture, etc., contains coins and medals, clean.

1870 1875, April, 8, 9, Bangs ; books, 1 lot medals, clean.

1871 1875, Dec. 17-28, Leavitt ; Oriental collection, contains coins and medals, clean.

1872 1875, Dec. 22, Birch ; Curiosities, 1 lot coins.

1873 1876, Jan. 17, etc., Dead Letter Office sale : contains coins and medals, clean.

1874 1876, Feb. 2, Davis & Harvey ; coins and medals, broadside, clean.

1875 1876, Feb. 10, 11, Leavitt ; 1 lot medals, clean.

1876 1876, Dec. 14, Leavitt ; contains coins.

1877 1876, Dec. 14-16, Barker : Japanese collection, several lots coins.

1878 1876, Dec. 19, 20, Leavitt ; Japanese curios, 2 lots coins.

1879 1877, Nov. 19-21, Cogniat ; coins and medals, clean.

1880 1878, Oct. 29, 30, Leavitt; books, 1 lot Lincoln medals.

1881 1878, Dec. 11, 12, Leavitt ; curios, 1 lot coins.

1882 1879, July 17, Birch ; autographs and coins.

1883 1879, Jan. 22, 23, Chas. F. Libbie: Massoll collection, coins and medals, clean.

1884 1879, Feb. 15, Leavitt : curios, 1 lot coins, clean.

1885 1879, Dec. 15, etc., Dead Letter Office sale; contains coins and medals, clean.

1886 1880, Oct. 26, 27, Leavitt : Palmer collection, several lots coins, clean.

1887 1882, Dec. 4, etc., Dead Letter Office sale; contains coins and medals, clean.

1888 1883, Feb. 14, Edwin Forrest sale, Phila., with supplementary priced catalogue, containing several lots medals and coins, clean.

∫ 1889 1883, Feb. 14, 15, Smith Library, contains 12 lots Lincoln medals, clean.

, *O* 1890 1883, May 29, Remsen collection; medals and coins, 1 sheet, clean.

∫ - 1891 Oct. 7. Palmer collection; stone implements, several lots coins, clean.

∪ - 1892 1876, N. Y. Aquarium Journal, contains a comic article and illustrations on the Japanese itzebu, clean.

PATTERN PIECES.

ↆ *Ɔ* 1893 1792 Martha Washington half disme. Female bust to the left. LIB. PAR. OF SCIENCE & INDURTRY. Rev. Flying eagle. UNITED STATES OF AMERICA. Very good ; *rare.*

∫ ↆ - 1894 1792 Eagle on a rock. TRIAL PIECE DESIGNED FOR UNITED STATES CENT. Copper ; very fine. 18.

ↄ *ↄ* 1895 Liberty cap in rays. Rev. FIRST STEAM COINAGE FEB. 22, 1836. Brass ; fine. 17.

ↄ) 1896 Same obverse. Rev. FIRST STEAM COINAGE MARCH 23, 1836. Bronzed copper ; proof. 17.

O 1897 Dupl'te of last No. Thin planchet : bronze ; v. fine. 17.

ↄ 1898 Half dollar, 1838. Head of Liberty to left : thirteen stars near border. Rev. Flying eagle to left. UNITED STATES OF AMERICA. HALF DOLLAR. Cracked die. *Silver :* proof ; *rare.*

1899 Cent, 1850. U. S. A. ONE TENTH SILVER. Nickel, very fine. 11.

1900 Same as last, but round hole in centre : *silvered,* very fine. 11.

1901 Cent without date : CENT ONE TENTH SILVER. Rev. UNITED STATES OF AMERICA. *Silver :* proof. 11.

1902 Three Cents, 1850 ; Liberty Cap in rays. Rev. III in wreath : UNITED STATES OF AMERICA. *Silver :* proof : very rare.

1903 Cent. 1851. Liberty seated. 13 stars near border. Rev. I CENT in wreath of oak. *Copper ;* uncirculated.

1904 Cent. 1853. Head of Liberty to left : 13 stars near border. Rev. ONE CENT in wreath of laurel. *Nickel ;* uncirculated. 11.

1905 Duplicate of last number. Uncirculated.

1906 Cent. 1854. Head of Liberty. *Copper*; unc. 16.

1907 Cent. 1855. Flying Eagle. *Nickel*; nearly proof. 16.

1908 Duplicate of last number. *Nickel*, proof, small scratch on obv.

1909 The same. *Copper*; very fine.

1910 Set of Cents. 1858. Large flying eagle, small flying eagle, Indian head, each combined with four different reverses, forming a perfect and complete set of 12 pieces. *Nickel*; proofs, very rare.

1911 Half Dollar. 1859. Head of Liberty to right. UNITED STATES OF AMERICA. Rev. 50 CENTS, ½ DOLLAR, and HALF DOLLAR in heavy wreath, making 3 combinations. *Silver*; proof. 3 pieces

1912 Duplicate Set. *Silver*; dull proofs. 3 pieces

1913 Another. *Copper*; dull proofs. 3 pieces

1914 Same obverse. Rev. Eagle, a shield on his breast and scroll in his beak. UNITED STATES OF AMERICA. HALF DOLLAR. *Silver*; proof.

1915 Half Dollar. 1859. Goddess of Liberty with shield and fasces seated to left, 13 stars near border. Rev. Same as last reverse. *Silver*; proof.

1916 The same design. *Copper*; proof.

1917 Another. *Bronze*; uncirculated.

1918 Nickel Cent. 1859. Rev. Oak-wreath and broad shield. Proof.

1919 Nickel Cent. 1859. Rev. Oak-wreath and narrow shield. Proof.

1920 Ten Dollars. 1862. Rev. GOD OUR TRUST on label. *Bronze*; uncirculated.

1921 Ten Dollars. 1862. Rev. GOD OUR TRUST in the field. *Bronze*; uncirculated.

1922 Half Dollar. 1862. Rev. GOD OUR TRUST on label. *Silver*; proof.

1923 Half Dollar. 1862. Rev. GOD OUR TRUST in the field. *Silver*; proof.

1924 Half Dollar. 1863. Rev. GOD OUR TRUST in the field. *Bronzed copper*; uncirculated.

1925 Ten dollars. 1863. Rev. GOD OUR TRUST on label. *Bronze*; uncirculated.

1926 Ten Dollars. 1863. Rev. GOD OUR TRUST in the field. *Bronze*; uncirculated.

1927 Two Cents, 1863. Bust of Washington, GOD AND OUR COUNTRY. Rev. 2 CENTS in wreath of wheat. *Copper :* uncirculated.

1928 Two Cents, 1863. The adopted design. *Copper :* proof.

1929 Cent. 1863. Indian head. Rev. Oak-wreath and narrow shield. *Nickel ;* proof.

1930 The same. *Copper ;* proof.

1931 The same. *Bronze ;* uncirculated.

1932 The same. Brass; uncirculated.

1933 Two cents. 1864. *Nickel ;* proof.

1934 Half dollar. 1865. Rev. IN GOD WE TRUST on label. *Copper ;* proof.

1935 Three cents. 1865. *Copper ;* proof.

1936 Three dollars. 1866. Indian head to left. Rev. 3 DOLLARS in wreath. *Nickel ;* uncirculated.

1937 Dollar. 1866. Rev. IN GOD WE TRUST on label. *Copper;* proof.

1938 Five cents. 1866. Bust of Washington to right. UNITED STATES AMERICA. Rev. 5 CENTS in wreath of laurel; IN GOD WE TRUST above. *Nickel :* proof.

1939 Five cents. 1866. Bust of Washington. IN GOD WE TRUST. Rev. 5 in a circle of 13 stars and rays, CENTS below. *Nickel ;* proof.

1940 Five Cents. 1866. Ornamental shield ; IN GOD WE TRUST above. Rev. 5 in a circle of thirteen stars, CENTS below. *Copper ;* proof.

1941 Five Cents. 1867. Same obv. Rev. 5 in wreath of laurel. Nickel : proof.

1942 Five Cents. 1867. Same obv. Rev. 5 in a circle of thirteen stars and rays. CENTS below. Nickel ; unc.

1943 Five Cents. 1867. Head of Liberty, with plain coronet. Rev. 5 CENTS in wreath of olive, IN GOD WE TRUST above. Nickel ; proof.

1944 Five cents. 1868. Head of Liberty, a star on coronet. Rev. V in wreath of laurel, IN GOD WE TRUST, on label, and Maltese cross above. *Nickel :* pr.

1945 5. 3, and 1 cents. 1868. Head of Liberty. Rev. V, III and I in wreath of laurel. *Nickel ;* proof.   3 pcs

1946 Five cents. 1868. Head of Liberty, plain coronet. Rev. 5 CENTS in wreath of olive, IN GOD WE TRUST, above. *Nickel ;* proof.

1947 5, 3, and 1 cents. 1869. Head of Liberty. Rev. V, III, and I in wreath of laurel. *Nickel ;* proof.   3 pcs

1948 Duplicate set. *Nickel*; proof. 2 pieces.

1949 1869 Set of pattern half dollar, quarter dollar, and
dime, standard silver, in three beautiful designs of
each denomination, making up a set of nine pieces;
complete. *Silver*, proof. Rare.

1950 1870. Similar set. *Silver*; proofs. Rare. 9 pieces.

1951 Mint of the United States. Annual Assay medal, 1869.
Bronze proof. 21.

1952 Annual Assay medal. 1861. Bronze; proof. 21.

1953 Annual Assay medal. 1870. Aluminum; proof, *rare*. 21.

1954 Annual Assay medal. 1871. Silver; proof, *rare*. 21.

1955 1848. Five Dollars, O mint, and 2½ dol. Brass. 2 ps.

POSTAL AND FRACTIONAL CURRENCY.

All new and in perfect condition.

1956 First issue. Postal Currency. 10 cts., without A. B.
Co.; uncirculated.

1957 The same. 5, 10, 25 and 50 cts., with A. B. Co.; uncirculated. 4 pieces

1958 The same. 5, 10, 25 and 50 cts., perforated edges; uncirculated. 4 pieces

1959 Second issue. Fractional Currency. Washington in
gilt oval, without date on back. 5, 10, 25 cts., uncirculated. 3 pieces

1960 Second issue. Fractional currency. Same design, with
date on back. 5, 10, 25, 50 cts.; uncirculated. 4 ps

1961 Third issue. 3, 5, 10, 25, 50 cts. Green backs. Uncirculated. 6 pieces

1962 Third issue. 25 cts. Fessenden. 50 cts. Justice; date
in gold on back. Uncirculated. 2 pieces

1963 Third issue. 50 cts. Spinner. Green back of new design; uncirculated, *very rare*.

1964 Third issue. 5, 10, 25, 50 and 50 cts. Red backs; uncirculated. 5 pieces

1965 Third issue. 10 cts. Washington. Red back; autograph signatures of Colby and Spinner. Uncirculated, *rare*.

1966 Third issue. 50 cts. Spinner. Red back; autograph
signatures of Colby and Spinner. Uncirculated, *rare*.

1967 Third issue. 50 cts. Justice. Red back; autograph
signatures of Colby and Spinner. Uncirculated, *rare*.

1968 Fourth issue. 10, 15, 25, 50 cts. ; silk threads in paper. Uncirculated.   4 pieces
1969 Fourth issue. 10, 15, 25, 50 cts. ; plain paper. Uncirculated.   4 pieces
1970 Fifth issue. 10 cts., Meredith; 50 cts., Dexter. Green seal. Uncirculated.   2 pieces
1971 Sixth issue. 10 cts., Meredith ; 25 cts., Walker; 50 cts., Crawford ; red Treasury seal. 10 and 25 cts., uncirculated. 50 cts., (good).   3 pieces
1972 50 Cents. Stanton. Red seal, uncirculated.
1973 Two backs of the 50 cent note on one sheet, second issue, printed in orange.

CONTINENTAL PAPER MONEY.

1974 1775, May 10. $6 ; very good.
1975 1775, Nov. 29. $3, 5, 6, and 8 ; good to fine.   4 pieces
1976 1776, Feb. 17. $⅙ A, $⅓ A, B, $⅔ A, B, $½, A. B. C. ; good, scarce.   8 pieces
1977 1778, Sept. 26. $5, 7, 8, 20, 30, 40, 50, and 60 ; good to fine. 8 pieces.

COLONIAL PAPER MONEY.

MASSACHUSETTS.

1978 1780, May 5. $1, 2, 3, 4, 5, 7, and 8 ; uncirculated, scarce.   7 pieces

RHODE ISLAND.

1979 1780, July 2. $5 : uncirculated and very rare.
1980 1780, July 2. $7 : uncirculated and very rare.
1981 1780, July 2. $8 : uncirculated and very rare.
1982 1789, July 2. $20 : uncirculated and very rare.

NEW JERSEY.

1983 1759, April 10. 30 sh. : poor, scarce.
1984 1760, April 12. 15 sh. ; poor, scarce.
1985 1762, April 8. £3, 15 sh. : fair, scarce.
1986 1763, Dec. 31. 1 sh., 18d., A B C D ; 3 sh., A B ; 6 sh., A B : 12 sh., A B : 15 sh. : uncirculated. 12 pieces
1987 1776, March 25. 18d., 3 sh., 12 sh. ; very fine. 3 pieces

PENNSYLVANIA.

1988 1757, March 10. 15 sh. Printed by B. Franklin and
D. Hall ; poor, rare.

1989 1772, April 3. 1 sh.; 18d. A B ; 2 sh., A B ; 2 sh. 6d ;
40 sh., D ; very fine. 7 pieces

1990 1769, March 10. 18d., 2 sh.; poor. 2 pieces

1991 1773, Oct. 1. 1 sh. 6d., 2 sh., 5 sh., 15 sh., 20 sh., 50 sh.;
fine. 6 pieces

1992 1775, July 20. 10 sh., A B; 20 sh., A B ; 30 sh., A B ;
40 sh.; very fine. 7 pieces

1993 1775, Oct. 25. 2 sh., 5 sh.; good. 2 pieces

1994 1776, April 25. 1 sh., 1 sh. 6d., 2 sh., 2 sh. 6d., 10 sh.,
A B; 20 sh., A B ; 30 sh., A. B ; 40 sh.; good to uncirculated, scarce. 11 pieces

1995 1776, April 25. 8d., B C; 4d., A B C; 6d., B C; 9d.,
A B C ; good to uncirculated, scarce. 10 pieces

1996 1777, April 10. Black Notes ; 4 sh., 1 sh. 6d., 2 sh., 3 sh.,
4 sh., 6 sh., 8 sh., 12 sh., 16 sh., 20 sh., 40 sh., £4; fine.
12 pieces

1997 1777, April 10. Black Notes ; 3d., 4d., 6d., 9d. ; letters
A B C each. Good to uncirculated. 12 pieces

1998 1777, April 10. Red Notes; 4 sh., 6 sh., 12 sh., 16 sh.,
20 sh., £4 ; very fine. 6 pieces

DELAWARE.

1999 1746, Feb. 28. Printed by B. Franklin ; 15 sh., 20
sh.; A. B.; poor and rare. 3 pieces

2000 1758, March 1. Franklin & Hall ; 20 sh. ; poor, scarce.

2001 1758, May 1. Franklin & Hall ; 15 sh., 20 sh. ; poor,
scarce. 2 pieces

2002 1759, June 1. Franklin & Hall, 20 sh.; fair, scarce.

2003 1776, Jan. 1. 1 sh., 1 sh. 6d., 2 sh. 6d., 4 sh., 5 sh., 6 sh.,
10 sh., 20 sh.; fine to uncirculated. 8 pieces

2004 1777, May 1. 20 sh.; fine.

MARYLAND.

2005 1770, March 1. $⅓, ⅓, ½, ⅔, 1, 2, 4, 6, 8; poor to good.
9 pieces

2006 1774, Apr. 10. $2, 4, 6 ; fine, scarce. 3 pieces

2007 1774, Dec. 7. $⅓, 1, 1½, 6, 8 ; fair to good. 5 pieces

2008 1776, Aug. 14. $⅓, 4 ; good. 2 pieces

2009 1776, Oct. 7, $6 ; fine and scarce.

2010 1775, June 1. Large notes, £5, 10, 20, very fair : rare.
3 pieces

2011 1776, March 6. £15, 20 ; fair and good, rare. 2 pieces

2012 1776, Dec. 23. $6 : very fine ; scarce.

2013 1778, Apr. 10. 2 sh. 6d., 3 sh. 9d, 5 sh., 10s. ; uncirculated.
4 pieces

CONFEDERATE NOTES AND BONDS.

The H Nos. correspond to the Nos. in Haseltine's Descriptive Catalogue of Confederate Notes and Bonds.

1861.

2014 H No. 1. $1000. Montgomery. Head of John C. Calhoun in lower left corner : head of Andrew Jackson in lower right corner. National Bank Note Co. Letter A. In very good condition, very rare.

ISSUE OF JULY 25, 1861.

2015 H No. 7. $100. Letter C. Two females in centre. Uncirculated, scarce.

2016 H No. 8. $50. Letter Bb. Head of Washington in centre ; uncirculated, rare.

2017 H No. 9. $20. Letter D. Uncirculated : rare.

2018 H No. 10. $20. Letter A. Fac-simile. Good condition : scarce.

SEPTEMBER 2, 1861.

2019 H No. 14. $100. A 5 A. Uncirculated : scarce.

2020 H No. 16. $50. A A. Uncirculated : scarce.

2021 H No. 20. $50. Head of Davis. Letter W A A W. No series, very fine.

2022 H No. 21. $20. Head of Stephens in lower left corner. 1st series 9. Very fine.

2023 H No. 21. $20. Head of Stephens in lower left corner. Third series. Nos. 1 to 10 complete. Very fine.
10 notes

2024 H No. 25. $20. Ship in centre. All different serial letters. Good to very fine.   4 notes

2025 H No. 26. $20. Flourishes Nos. 25 and 26. Very fine.   2 notes

2026 H No. 27. $20. No flag on mainmast. No serial. Nos. 20, 23, 24, and 26. Very fine.   4 notes

2027 H No. 29. $20. Female and globe, partly red, rare. Engraved by the Southern Bank Note Co. Letter A. Good, very rare.

2028 H No. 30. $10. Negro picking cotton. Letter F. Good.

2029 H No. 31. $10. Gen. Marion. Second series. No. 5. Very good.

2030 H No. 32. $10. Head of Hunter. Letter J. Very fine.

2031 H No. 33. $10. Group of Indians in centre, partly red. Letter C. Rare.

2032 H No. 36. $10. Two females and urn. No. 14. Good.

2033 H No. 37. $10. Same design. Hoyer & Ludwig. No. 15. Very good.

2034 H No. 38. $10. Head of Hunter. No Series. Letters W X Y Z. Complete, uncirculated.   4 notes

2035 H No. 40½. $10. Same design. No series. Letter Y. Uncirculated.

2036 H No. 42. $5. Group of females in centre. Letter C. Very good. Rare.

2037 H No. 45. $5. Sailor in centre. Letter A. Very good.

2038 H No. 48. $5. Head of Memminger in centre. Letter X. Fine.

2039 H No. 50. $5. Same design. Partly green. Letter K. Uncirculated.

2040 H No. 53. $5. Female seated on a bale of cotton. J. T. Paterson & Co. No series. Nos. 9 to 16. Very fine to uncirculated.   8 notes

2041 H No. 53. $5. The same as preceding. Second series. Nos. 9 to 16. Fine to uncirculated.   8 notes

2042 H No. 54. $2. The South striking down the North and crippling the eagle in the centre. First series. No. 2. Fair, very rare.

1862

2043 H No. 55. $100. Interest notes. Negroes hauling cotton. Letters W X Y and Z. Very fine.   4 notes

2044 H No. 55. $100. Same design as preceding but very much smaller text. Letters W X Y Z. Very fine and contained by Hoyer & Co.   4 notes

2045 H No. 56. $100. Interest notes. Train of cars.
Letters A to H complete. Fine to uncirculated. 8 notes

2046 H No. 57. $100. Same as preceding, smaller serial
letters. Letters A to H. Fine to unc. 8 notes

2047 H No. 58. $100. Letters A C D. Very fine. 3 notes

2048 H No. 59. $100. Letters A B C D E G H. Very
fine. 7 notes

2049 H No. 60. $100. Letters A to H complete. Very
fine. 8 notes

2050 H No. 62. $100. Letters A A, A A b to A A h com-
plete. Fine to uncirculated. 8 notes

JUNE 2, 1862.

2051 H No. 63. $2. First series. Nos. 1, 3, 4, 5, 6, 7, 8, 9,
10. Good. 9 notes

2052 H No. 63. $2. Second series. Nos. 1 to 10 complete.
Very good. 10 notes

2053 H No. 63. $2. Third series. Nos. 1 to 12 complete.
Fine. 12 notes

2054 H No. 64. $2. " 2 " and " Two " in green across the
face. Second series. Nos. 3, 7, 9, 10. Fair; scarce.
4 notes

2055 H No. 65. $1. Steamship in centre. 1st series. Nos. 6,
7, 8. Fair. 3 notes

2056 H No. 65. $1. Same design. Second series. Nos. 1
to 10. Good. 10 notes

2057 H No. 65. $1. Same design. Third series. Nos. 1 to
12. Good. 12 notes

2058 H No. 66. $1. Same, but has " 1 " and " ONE " in
green across the face. Second series. Nos. 1, 5;
good, scarce. 2 notes

SEPTEMBER 2, 1862.

2059 H No. 67. $10. Female seated on a barrel. Letter P.
Very fine.

DECEMBER 2, 1862.

2060 H No. 68. $100. Head of Mrs. Davis. No series.
Letter D. Very good, scarce.

2061 H No. 71. $20. 1st series. Letter B. Uncirculated.

2062 H No. 74. $10. No series. Letter B. Uncirculated.

2063 H No. 74. $10. 2d series. Letters A to H complete.
Very fine. 8 notes

2064 H No. 75. **#10. 2d series. Letters A to H complete.
Very fine. 8 notes

2065 H No. 77. 2d series. Letters A to H complete; uncirculated. 8 notes

2066 H No. 80. $5. 1st series. Letter F. Very fine.

2067 H No. 80. $5. 2d series. Letter A. Very fine.

2068 H No. 81. $2. No series. Letter A. Good.

2069 H No. 82. $2. 1st series. B C D E F H I. Fair. 7 no.

2070 H No. 82. $2. Variety not mentioned by Haseltine. (dots after serial letters.) 1st series. Letters B C D F G H I. Fair. 7 notes

2071 H No. 83. $1. No series. Letter A. Very fine.

2072 H No. 84. $1. 1st series. Letters B to I complete. Very good. 8 notes

2073 H No. 85. $1. 1st series. Letters B to I complete. Fine. 8 notes

APRIL 6, 1863.

2074 H No. 86. $100. Head of Mrs. Davis. 1st series. Letters A D. Uncirculated. 2 notes

2075 H No. 88. $50. Head of Jeff. Davis. 1st series. Letter Z. Uncirculated.

2076 H No. 90. $20. 1st series. Letter H. Very fine.

2077 H No. 91. $20. 1st series. Letters A to H complete. Very fine. 8 notes

2078 H No. 91. $20. 2d series. Letter F. Fine.

2079 H No. 91. $20. 3d series. Letters A to H complete. Uncirculated. 8 notes

2080 H No. 92. $10. No series. Letters A B C H. Very fine. 4 notes

2081 H No. 93. $10. 1st series, large type. Letters A to H. Uncirculated. 8 notes

2082 H No. 93. $10. 1st series, small type. Letter A. Unc.

2083 H No. 93. $10. 2d series, large type. Letters A to H. Very fine. 8 notes

2084 H No. 97. $5. No series. Letters A to H. Very fine. 8 notes

2085 H No. 98. $5. 1st series. Letters A to H. Very fine. 8 notes

2086 H No. 98. $5. 2d series, small type. Letters A to H. Very fine. 8 notes

2087 H No. 98. $5. 2d series, large type. Letter C. Fine.

2088 H No. 101. $2. 1st series. Letters A to H. Good. 8 notes

2089 H No. 104. $2. 2d series. Letters A to H. Good.
8 notes

2090 H No. 105. $1. No series. Letters A to H. Fine.
8 notes

2091 H No. 105. $1. 2d series. Letters A to H. Fine.
8 notes

2092 H No. 106. $1. No series. Letters C D F H. Good.
4 notes

2093 H No. 108. $1. No series. Letters A to H. Fine.
8 notes

2094 H No. 108. $1. 2d series. Letters A to H. Good.
8 notes

2095 H No. 109. $1. 1st series. Letters A to H. Good.
8 notes

2096 H No. 109. $1. 2d series. Letters A to H. Good.
8 notes

2097 H No. 110. $1. 2d series. Letter F. Good.

2098 H No. 111. $1. 2d series. Letter B. Fair.

2099 H No. 112. 50c. 1st series. Letters A to I. Uncirculated.
9 notes

2100 H No. 112. 50c. 2d series. Letters A to I. Uncirculated.
9 notes

FEBRUARY 17, 1864.

2101 H No. 113. $500. Letters A to D. Very fine. 4 notes

2102 H No. 114. $100. No series, series 1 and 11. Letters A to D complete. Uncirculated. 12 notes

2103 H No. 115. $100. No series, series 1 and 11. Letters A to D complete. Uncirculated 12 notes

2104 H No. 116. $50. No series, series 1, 2, 3, 4. Letters W to Z complete Uncirculated. 20 notes

2105 H No. 117. $20. No series to X series. Letters A to D complete. Uncirculated. 44 notes

2106 H No. 117. $20. XI series. Letters A to D. Uncirculated, scarce. 4 notes

2107 H No. 118. $10. No series to 10 series. Letters A to H complete. Uncirculated. 88 notes

2108 H No. 118. $10. Not in Haseltine. 3d series. Letter A C. Good.

2109 H No. 119. $5. No series to 7 series. Letters A to H complete, except 2 notes. Uncirculated. 62 notes

2110 H No. 119. $5. Not in Haseltine. No series. Letter C G. Fine.

2111 H No. 120. $2. No series. Letters A to H. Uncirculated.
8 notes

2112 H No. 124. $2. No series. Letters F and H. Very
good.   2 notes

2113 H No. 126. $2. No series. Letters A to H. Fine.
8 notes

2114 H No. 127. $2. Not in Hairline. Dots in front of
both letters. Letters A B C E F G H. Very good.
7 notes

2115 H No. 128. $1. No series. Letters A B C D F G H.
Good.   7 notes

2116 H No. 129. $1. No series. Letters A to H. Fine.
8 notes

2117 H No. 133. $1. No series. Letter D. Good.

2118 H No. 134. $1. No series. Letters A to H. Fine.
8 notes

2119 H No. 135. $1. No series. Letters A to H. Fine.
8 notes

2120 H No. 136. 50 cents. First series. Letters A to I.
Uncirculated.   9 notes

2121 H No. 136. 50 cents. Second Series. Letters A to I.
Uncirculated.   9 notes

2122 Feb. 17, '64. A $20 note, having a poem printed on
the back, beginning with " Representing nothing
on God's earth now," etc.

2123 A pen facsimile, very finely executed, of a 75 cent issue
of the City of Richmond, State of Virginia.

2124 Sept. 2nd, 1861. $20. Duplicates, assorted. Very fine.
8 notes

2125 1862. $100. Negroes hoeing. Assorted duplicates.
Fine.   20 notes

2126 1862. $100. Train of cars. Assorted duplicates.
fine.   35 notes

2127 June 2d, 1862. $2. Assorted duplicates. Good. 21 notes

2128 Dec. 2nd, 1862. $2. Assorted duplicates. Poor.
5 notes

2129 Dec. 2d, 1862. $1. Assorted duplicates. Fair. 6 notes
2130 April 6th, 1863. $2. Assorted duplicates. Good. 40 notes
2131 April 6th, 1863. $1. Assorted duplicates. Fair. 41 notes
2132 April 6th, 1863. 50 cents. Assorted duplicates. Poor.
7 notes

2133 Feb. 17th, 1864. $500. Assorted duplicates. Very
fine.   2 notes
2134 Feb. 17th, 1864. $100. Assorted duplicates. Fine
573 notes

3 2135 Feb. 17th, 1864. $50. Assorted duplicates. Good.
                                                    398 notes
3 2136 Feb. 17th, 1864. $20. Assorted duplicates. Good.
                                                    882 notes
1/4 2137 Feb. 17th, 1864. $10. Duplicates. Good. 2,252 notes
1/4 2138 Feb. 17th, 1864. $5. Duplicates. Good. 1,538 notes
3 2139 Feb. 17th, 1864. $2. Duplicates. Fine.   62 notes
3 2140 Feb. 17th, 1864. $1. Duplicates. Fine.   23 notes
3 2141 Feb. 17th, 1864. 50 cents. Duplicates. Fine. 10 notes
1 2142 Virginia, North Carolina, etc. Duplicates. Poor.
           147 notes.

CONFEDERATE BONDS.

2143 H No. 5. $100. Act of Congress, Feb. 28, 1861.
2144 H $50. Act of Congress, Feb. 28, 1861. Not in
      Haseltine.
2145 H No. 8. $29,000. Act of Congress, Aug. 19, 1861.
2146 H $50. Act of Congress, Aug. 19, 1861. Not in
      Haseltine.
2147 H $100. Act of Congress, Aug. 19, 1861. Not in
      Haseltine.
2148 H No. 30. $1,000. Act of Congress, Feb. 20, 1863.
      Blue paper.
2149 H No. 31. $1,000. Act of Congress, Feb. 20, 1863.
2150 H No. 33. $500. Act of Congress, Feb. 20, 1863.
2151 H No. 34. $500. Act of Congress, Feb. 20, 1863. Pink
      paper.
2152 H No. 36. $100. Act of Congress, Feb. 20, 1863.
2153 H $500. Act of Congress, March 23, 1863. Not in
      Haseltine.
2154 H $1,000. Act of Congress, March 23, 1863. Not in
      Haseltine.
2155 H No. 41. $1,000. Act of Congress, April 30, 1863.
2156 H No. 43. $1,000. Act of Congress, Feb. 17th, 1864.
      Second series.
2157 H No. 43. $1000. Act of Congress, Feb. 17, 1864.
      Eight series. Not in H.
2158 H $1000. Act of Congress, March 23, 1863. Call
      certificate, not in H.
2159 H No. 49. $100. Act of Congress, Feb. 17, 1864.
2160 Missouri Defence Bonds. $1, 3, 4, 4.50, 20, 50, 100.
      Not signed ; different designs ; uncirculated. 7 notes

STATE ISSUES.

VIRGINIA.

2161 $10. Oct. 15, 1861, Treasury note. Standing figure of Liberty on left. B ; very fine.

2162 $10. Oct. 15, 1861, Treasury notes. Seated female in centre, "X" and "Ten" in green. A B C D ; very fine. 4 pieces

2163 $5. March 13, 1862, Treasury notes. A B C D. Long notes ; very fine. 4 pieces

2164 $5. March 13, 1862, Treasury notes. A B C D. Short notes ; good. 4 pieces

2165 $1. May 15, 1862, Treasury notes. A B. Good. 2 pcs

2166 $1. July 21, 1862, Treasury notes. A B C D. Very good. 4 pieces

2167 $1. Oct. 21, 1862, Treasury notes. A B C D. Very good. 4 pieces

2168 10c. to $2. Notes issued by corporations, cities and towns ; all different, many rare ; poor to unc. 17 pcs

2169 15c. to $1. Notes issued by counties ; some rare, all different ; very good. 15 pieces

2170 5c. to $50. Notes issued by firms, etc. ; all different ; poor to good. 7 pieces

2171 25c. to $2. Notes issued by banking institutions ; all different ; very good. 9 pieces

NORTH CAROLINA.

2172 5c. and 20c. Oct. 1, 1861. Fair and fine ; very small. 2 notes

2173 10 cents. Oct. 1, 1861. No letter. B. Very small ; good. 2 notes

2174 25 cents. Oct. 1, 1861. No letter. Very small ; good.

2175 50 cents. Oct. 1, 1861. No letter. Very small ; good.

2176 10 cents. Sept. 1, 1862. Negro ploughing. No letter ; good.

2177 10 cents. Sept. 1, 1862. Bee-hive. Letters G, D. Very good. 2 pieces

2178 25 cents. Sept. 1, 1862. Different borders and varieties ; good to uncirculated, no duplicates. 9 notes

2179 50 cents. Sept. 1, 1862. Ship. Good to uncirculated, all different. 12 notes

2180 5 cents. Jan. 1, 1863. Females. A to U complete ; uncirculated. 21 notes

2181 10 cents. Jan. 1, 1863. Bee-hive. A to U complete; uncirculated.   21 notes

2182 25 cents. Jan. 1, 1863. A to U complete; uncirculated.   21 notes

2183 50 cents. Jan. 1, 1863. Ship, letters to right; fine.   12 notes

2184 50 cents. Jan. 1, 1863. Ship, letters to left; fine.   9 notes

2185 75 cents. Jan. 1, 1863. Different letters; fine to uncirculated.   12 notes

2186 25 cents. Jan. 1, 1864. Different letters; mostly uncirculated.   8 notes

2187 50 cents. Jan. 1, 1864. Different letters; mostly uncirculated.   14 notes

2188 $1. Oct. 1, 3, 4, 5, 1861. Very good.   4 notes

2189 $1. Oct. 10 to 21. A and B of each date; fine. 24 notes

2190 $1. Sept. 1, 1862. Wide notes, A to E; fine. 5 notes

2191 $1. Jan. 1, 1863. Varieties; fine.   2 notes

2192 $2. Oct. 1, 1861. Letters A B D; very good. 3 notes

2193 $2. Oct. 2, 1861. Letters A B C D; very fine. 4 notes

2194 $2. Oct. 4, 1861. Letters A B C D E. Uncirculated.   5 notes

2195 $2. Oct. 6, 1861. Letters A B C D E. Uncirculated.   5 notes

2196 $2. Jan. 1, 1863. Letters A to K. M. Uncirculated.   12 notes

2197 $3. Jan. 1, 1863. Letter E. Large note. Uncir. Rare.

2198 $5. 1862 and 1863. Written dates. Steamship. Very fine. All different.   4 notes

2199 $10. 1862. Written dates. Train of cars. Letters A G. Uncirculated, rare.   2 notes

2200 50 cents and $1. Greensboro Mutual Ins. Co. Four varieties, good.   4 notes

SOUTH CAROLINA.

2201 50 cents. July 1, 1861. Bank of the State of S. C. Fine, very rare.   1 note

2202 25 and 50 cents, June, 1862. Bank of the State of S. C. Fair.   2 notes

2203 25 and 50 cents. Feb. 1, 1863. Bank of the State of S C. Fine.   2 notes

2204 5 and 50 cents. 1862, 1864. Individual notes. Fair.   2 notes

GEORGIA.

2205 25, 50 cents, and $2. Jan. 1, 1863. Different letters. Good to uncirculated. Scarce. 6 notes

2206 $10. Feb. 1, 1863. Letter A. Uncirculated. scarce.

2207 $1 and 4. Jan. 1, 1864. Good. scarce. 2 notes

2208 $5, 10, 20, 50, 100. April 6, 1864. Different letters. Good to fine. 10 notes

2209 5 cents to $10. Notes issued by Banking Co.'s. Fair to uncirculated, many rare, all different, a desirable lot. 35 notes

2210 5 cents to $1. Western & Atlantic R. R. Good. 4 pieces

FLORIDA.

2211 25 and 50 cents. February 2nd, 1863. Denominations in blue. Fine. 2 notes

ALABAMA.

2212 10c, 25c, 50c, $1. Jan. 1, 1863. Different arms and letters. Good to uncirculated. 15 notes.

2213 $5. Jan. 1, 1864. Horseman. Letter D.

2214 5c, $1, $2. 1862 and 1863. Mobile and Selma notes. Very fine. 3 notes

MISSISSIPPI.

2215 $1, 2.50. May 1, 1862. "Cotton pledged." Very good. 2 notes

2216 $10. July 1, 1862. "Faith of the State pledged." Very good.

LOUISIANA.

2217 $5. October 10, 1862. South striking down the eagle and treading on the eagle. Very good and scarce.

2218 $5. March 10, 1863. Same design. Very good. scarce.

TEXAS.

2219 50 cents. October 23, 1862. County warrant. Fine, rare.

2220 50 cents. April 12, 1863. County warrant. Fine, rare.

TENNESSEE.

2221 10 cents to $3. 1861 to 1863. Bank notes. Very fine. 7 notes

2222 Catalogues and price lists of Colonial and Confederate notes, etc. All priced except three. 14 pieces

NUMISMATIC LIBRARY.

The largest and finest collection of American and Foreign Works on Numismatology and kindred subjects ever offered in the United States. Besides finely-bound copies of standard Foreign Works on English, Scotch, Irish, French, Dutch, German, Russian and Ancient Coinages, this Collection contains a large number of rare American publications on our Colonial and National Coinages. The opportunity to purchase herewith offered is one that cannot occur again in the immediate future, and will, it is hoped, be the occasion of a goodly gathering of buyers of Coin Books and Americana.

2223 ADDISON. C. G. The Knights Templars . . . . . enlarged by Robert Macoy. New York, 1873. 8° half mor. Roman coins. pp 43-46.

2224 ADDISON, Joseph. Works. New York, 1853. Vol. II containing Dialogues upon the usefulness of ancient medals. 12° 9 pls H'f mor. by Bradstreet

2225 The same. London, 1726. Vol. III. containing the Dialogues. 16° 31 pls calf.

2226 AKERMAN, John Yonge. A numismatic manual: or guide to the study of Greek, Roman and English coins. London, 1832. 16° 7 pls

2227 The same. A descriptive catalogue of rare and unedited Roman coins. London, 1834. 2 vols. 8° h'f mor Numerous plates

2228 The same. Coins of the Romans relating to Britain. London, 1836. 16° 6 pls

2229 The same. [Second edition.] London, 1844. 8° 6 pls full mor.

2230 The same. Catalogue d'une partie de la collection de médailles du chevalier de Horta. Londres. 1839. 8° Greek and Roman coins.

2231 The same. A list of tokens issued by Wiltshire Tradesmen in the seventeenth century. London. 1849. 8° 1 pl

2232 The same. Ancient coins of cities and princes. Hispania, Gallia, Britannia. London. 1846. 8° 24 pls full mor.

2233 The same. An introduction to the study of ancient and modern coins. London. 1848. 16° calf

2234 The same. Tradesmen's tokens, current in London and its vicinity between the years 1648 and 1672. London. 1849. 4° 8 pls large paper.

2235 AMERICAN Stamp Mercury and Numismatist. Boston, 1867–1870. 4 vols. in 1. 4° h f mor.

2236 ANDREAS, Valerius. Imagines doctorum virorum e variis gentibus. Antverpiae, 1611. 24° num. ills.

2237 ANDREW, W. The habits, customs, and antiquities of the Romans. London. 1848. 12° Roman coins, p 34.

2238 ANNAEUS FLORUS. Recensitus et illustratus a Joanne Georgio Graevio. Trajecti Batavorum, 1680. 12° Num. ills. of Roman coins.

2239 ANSELL, Geo. F. The Royal Mint: its working, conduct, and operations, fully and practically explained. London. 1870. 4° illns of coins, etc.

2240 AXTHON, Charles E. Silver Louis of fifteen sous, struck under Louis XIV, for circulation in French America. no title page 8° h f mor.

2241 ANTIQUARIAN. A review of the article on Continental money in Harper's Magazine for March, 1869. 8° h f mor.

2242 APPLETON, Wm. S. Description of a selection of coins and medals relating to America. Cambridge. 1870. 8°

2243 The same. Description of Medals of Washington in his collection. Boston. 1873. Large 8° 24 pp paper cover. Rare.

2244 ARBUTHNOT, Charles. Tables of ancient coins, weights and measures, explained and exemplified. London. 1727. 4° 18 tables.

2245 ARCHAEOLOGICAL Journal. London, 1846–48. Vols. I to V. Contains several papers on coins.

2246 ARCHAEOLOGIST (The) and Journal of Antiquarian Science. Nos. I to X. Lond. 1842. 8° cl.

2247 ATTINELLI, E. J. Numisgraphics, or a list of catalogues in which occur coins or medals. New York. 1876. 4° large paper, of which only 12 copies were printed.

2248 AURELIUS VICTOR. Historiae Romanae breviarium. Trajecti ad Rhenum. 1696. 12° num. ills. of coins.

2249 ☒——. W. A manual of Roman coins from the earliest period to the extinction of the empire. London. 1865. 8° cl 21 pls

2250 BARNUM. Catalogue or Guide Book of Barnum's American Museum. New York. 1853. 16° h'f mor. Coins, etc. pp 18, 37, 60. Rare.

2251 BAGG, S. C. The antiquities and legends of Durham. Read before the Numismatic and Antiquarian Soc. of Montreal. 1866. 8° Rare.

2252 BANKERS' MAGAZINE. Edited by I. Smith Homans. Baltimore and New York, 1847 to 1871. 85 nos. and 1 bound volume (1854–55), incomplete. Contains numerous papers on coins, etc. Very scarce.

2253 BARRA, E. I. Something about coins. San Francisco. 1863. 24°

2254 BEAUVAIS. An essay on the means of distinguishing antique from counterfeit coins and medals. Translated from the French by J. T. Brochett. Newcastle, 1819. 12° h'f mor.

2255 BIE. Jacques de. La France metallique contenant les actions célèbres tant publiques que privées des Rois et Reynes, remarquées en leurs médailles d'or, argent et bronze. Paris, 1636. f° 131 pls *Also* Les Familles de la France illustrées par les monument des médailles anciennes et modernes. Paris. 1636. f° [47] pls. Together in 1 vol. calf. Best edition.

"The prints of Jacob Van Bie rank with the works of the best old Flemish engravers."—SPOONER.

2256 BIRCH, S. New coins of British Reguli. 8° 1 pl Reprinted from the Numismatic Chronicle. Vol. XIV.

2257 The same. Notes on some types of Tarentum. Observations on some unedited coins of Asia Minor. 8° 1 pl. Reprinted from Numismatic Chronicle. Vol. VII.

2258 The same. Notes on Types of Caulonia. On the types of Verina. 8° Reprinted from Numismatic Chronicle.

2259 BIZOT, P. Histoire metallique de la Republique de Hollande. Amsterdam. 1688–90. 3 vols. 12° num. ills. h'f calf.

2260 BARRELL, M. The numismatist. London 1851. 8° Pts I and II, all published.

2261 BOTTKOWSKI, Alexander. Dictionnaire numismatique.
Médailles romaines impériales et grecques coloniales.
Leipzig. 1877–81. Pts 1 and 2 of Vol. I complete.
A valuable work on Romer coins, with the degree of rarity and price
of each piece.

2262 BOWRING, Sir John. The decimal system in numbers,
coins, and accounts. London, 1854. 12° pls.

2263 BOYD, Andrew. A memorial Lincoln bibliography:
being an account of books, eulogies, sermons, portraits, engravings, MEDALS, etc. Albany, 1870. Portrait. 8°

2264 BOYNE, W. Tokens issued in the seventeenth century
in England, Wales, and Ireland. London, 1858. 42
pls. Thick 8° cl.

2265 The same. Another large paper copy. 4° cl.

2266 The same. Tokens issued in the seventeenth, eighteenth,
and nineteenth centuries in Yorkshire. Headingley,
privately printed for the author. 1858. 4° cl 14 pls

2267 The same. The silver tokens of Great Britain and Ireland, the dependencies and colonies. London, 1866.
Printed for subscribers only. 4° 7 pls cl.

2268 BRECK, Samuel. Historical sketch of Continental Paper
Money. Phila. 1863. 8°

2269 BURN, J. H. A descriptive catalogue of the London
traders, tavern, and coffee-house tokens current in
the seventeenth century. Second edition. London,
1855. 8° cl. very scarce.

2270 BUSHNELL, Chas. I. An historical account of the first
three business tokens issued in N. Y. N. Y., 1859.
12° h'f mor 1 pl

2271 The same. An arrangement of Tradesmen's Cards, political tokens, etc. N. Y. 1858. 8° h'f mor 4 pls

2272 CAMDEN'S Britannia, newly translated into English. London, 1695. f ills of coins.

2273 CARDONNEL, Adam de. Numismata Scotiae, or a series
of the Scottish coinage. Edinburgh, 1786. 4° 20 pls

2274 CARDWELL, E. Lectures on the coinage of the Greeks
and Romans. Oxford, 1832. 8° cl

2275 CARROLL (Charles) of Carrollton, his medal. The
Catholic World. N. Y., 1877. July. 8° h'f mor Rare

2276 CARTER, Thomas. Medals of the British Army. London, 1861. 3 vols. in 1. 8° cl. 18 colored plates.

2277 The same. Vol. I. The Crimean Campaign. 8 pls.
colored.

2278 CHALON, R. Recherches sur les monnaies des Comtes de Namur. Suppléments. Bruxelles, 1870. 4° 2 pls.

2279 CHASE, P. E. Catalogue of tokens circulating during the Rebellion of 1861. n. p. n. d. 8° h'f mor.

2280 The same. Another copy, unbound.

2281 CHEVALIER, M. On the probable fall in the value of gold. N. Y., 1859. 8° cl.

2282 CHINESE coins. Folding plate of Chinese coins. 8° h'f mor.

2283 CHRISTMAS, Rev. H. Irish coins of copper and billon. London, 1862, 63. 2 pts 8° Reprinted from Numismatic Chronicle.

2284 The same. On Anglo-American copper coinage. Copper coinage of the British colonies in America. London, 1862. 2 pts Reprinted from Numismatic Chronicle. Very scarce.

2285 The same. Anglo-Gallic coins of copper and billon. Lond., 1863. Reprinted from Numismatic Chronicle.

2286 CLARKE, F. W. Weights, measures, and money of all nations. N. Y., 1876.

2287 CLARKE, WM. The connection of the Roman, Saxon, and English coins. London, 1771. 4°.

2288 CLAY, Charles. Currency of the Isle of Man. Douglas, 1869. 8° cl pls.

2289 CLEVELAND, C. D. A compendium of Grecian antiquities. Boston, 1831. 12° Coins, p 234. Rare.

2290 COGAN, Ed. Table of gold, silver, and copper coins *not* issued by the United States mint. New York, 1871. 8°.

2291 The same. American Store Cards, etc., with space for marking condition, etc. Philadelphia. 4° paper cover. Scarce.

2292 COLLAS, Achille. The authors of England. A series of medallion portraits. London, 1838. 4° 14 pls.

2293 COOKE, William. The Medallic History of Imperial Rome . . . with the several medals and coins accurately copied and curiously engraven. London, 1781. 2 vols. 4° 61 pls. Rare.

2294 CROSBY, S. S. Early coins of America. Boston, 1875. 4° Complete in parts, as issued, with plates. A valuable work.

2295 CRYSTAL Palace, New York, 1853. 12° h'f mor. Coins, etc., pp 79, 183.

2296 A Day in the N. Y. Crystal Palace. By W. C. Richards. N. Y., 1853. 12° cl Coins, etc., pp. 92, 102, 126, 166.

2297 DALTON, Charles. Catalogue of British war medals and other decorations. London, 1874. For private circulation. Rare.

2298 DAMETR, Hugues. Tableau du titre, poids et valeur des différentes monnaies d'or et d'argent qui circulent dans le commerce. Genève, 1807. 4° 50 pls.

2299 DE PEYSTER, J. Watts. Description of medals presented by H. R. M. Oscar King of Sweden and Norway, the Goths and Vandals, to Gen'l J Watts de Peyster n. p. n. d. 8° h'f mor. Very rare

2300 The same. The history of Carausius, the Dutch Augustus. Poughkeepsie, 1858. 8° h'f mor.

2301 DICKESON, M. W. The American Numismatic Manual. Third and best edition. Phila., 1865. 4° 21 pls Very scarce.

2302 DILLAWAY, Chas. K Roman antiquities, and ancient mythology. Boston, 1858. 12° pls

2303 DISOSWAY, G. P. A chapter on coins and medals—from the National Magazine. Nos. 1 and 2 of Vol. IV. 8° h'f mor.

2304 DOWLING, Rev. John. The history of Romanism. N. Y. 1845. 8 h'f mor. Medals, pp. 690, 682.

2305 DU BOIS, W. E. A brief account of the collection of coins belonging to the Mint of the United States. Philadelphia, 1846. 16 h'f mor. 1 pl.

2306 DU CHOUL, Guillaume. Discours sur la castrametation et discipline militaire des Romains. Lyon, 1556. 4° vellum. num. pls.

2307 DUMERSAN, M. Histoire du cabinet des médailles. Paris, 1838. 8 h'f mor

2308 ECKFELDT and DU BOIS. New varieties of gold and silver coins, and bullion. Phila., 1850. 12° ills.

2309 The same. Second edition. Phila., 1851. 8° cl. pls.

2310 The same. A manual of gold and silver coins of all nations struck within the past century, with supplement. Phila. 1842-52. 2 vols. h'f mor. pls. h'f mor.

2311 ECKE, J. A view of the gold and silver coins of all nations. London. n. d. sm. 4° 34 pls.

2312 EDWARDS, Edward. The Napoleon medals . . . engraved by the process of Achilles Collas. With historical and biographical notices. London, 1837. large f° 40 plates and frontisp.

2313 EMBLEMATA anniversaria academiae Altorfinae studiorum iuventutis exercitandorum causa proposita et variorum orationibus exposita. Norimbergae, 1597. sm 4° num. ills. of medals.

2314 ENGLISH coins. Ills. in the Trinity Magazine. 1836. f° h'f mor.

2315 ESSAY upon money and coins. London, 1757. 2 vols. 12° h'f mor.

2316 EVANS, John. The coins of the ancient Britons. London, 1864. 8° 17 pls cl.

2317 EVELYN, J. A Discourse of medals, antient and modern. London, 1797. f° num. ills.

2318 HELT, Joseph B. An historical account of Massachusetts currency. Boston, 1839. 8° h'f mor. pls

2319 FLEURIMONT, G. R. Médailles du règne de Louis XV. [Paris, 1748.] f° 78 pls and frontisp.

2320 FLIESSBACH, F. Münzsammlung enthaltend die wichtigsten seit dem Westphälischen Frieden bis zum jahre 1800. Leipzig, 1856. 8° 120 pls in relief.

2321 FOLKES, Martin. English coinage, silver and gold, faithfully copied from the originals. n. p. n. d. 4° h'f mor. 67 pls Last and best edition, published by the Society of Antiquaries in 1763.

2322 The same. A table of English silver and gold coins. London, 1745. 4° 42 pls

2323 FRANCIS, J. History of the Bank of England. First American edition, by I. Smith Homans, Jr. New York, 1862. 8°

2324 FRANKLIN medallion struck for the inauguration of the statue of Franklin. Boston, 1856. 8° 1 pl Rare.

2325 FRANKS, David. The New York Directory, containing tables of the different coins. N. Y., 1786. sm. 4° Reprinted 1874. h'f mor

2326 FROSSARD, Ed. Monograph of United States Cents and Half Cents. Irvington, 1879. 4° h'f mor. 9 pls

2327 FROST, John. American naval biography. Phila., 1844. 8° 5 pls of medals.

2328 GAGE, Wm. L. The Home of God's People. Hartford, Conn., 1872. 8° Ills. of Jewish coins, pp. 289-91. Rare.

2329 GOLDING, Charles. The coinage of Suffolk, consisting of regal coins, leaden pieces, and tokens. London. 1868. 4° cl. 6 pls

2330 GOWEN, Wm. M. A short history of paper money and banking in the U. S. New York. 1840. 8°

2331 GOTTEN. Catalogue of the coins of Canute. London. 1777. 4° 1 pl

2332 GOURDON de Genouillac, H. Dictionnaire historique des ordres de chevalerie créés chez les différents peuples depuis les premiers temps jusqu'à nos jours. 2d ed. Paris. 1860. 12° mm. ill.

2333 GRASSET, J. G. Th. Handbuch der alten Numismatik von den ältesten Zeiten bis auf Constantin d. Gr. Leipzig, 1854. 8° 72 pls in relief.

2334 GREEN, B. R. A lecture on the study of ancient coins, in connection with history. London. 1829. 8° 2 pls.

2335 The same. A numismatic Atlas of ancient history, with descriptive letter press. London. 1820. large f° 21 pls neatly colored by hand.

2336 GROUX, D. E. Prospectus of an important work, in three columns, to be called "Numismatical History of the U. S." Boston. 1856. 8° ill.

2337 HALLER, F. L. Catalogus numismatum veterum quae exstant in Museo civitatis Bernensis. Bernae. 1822. 12° 1 pl

2338 HANFFSTALER, G. Exercitationes faciles de nummis veterum pro tyronibus. Norimbergae. 1755. 4° 2 pls in 1 vol. num. pls

2339 HAGER, A. M. History of the issues of paper-money in the American colonies. St. Louis. 1854. 8° h-f mor. Rare.

2340 HASELTINE, J. W. Description of the paper money issued by the Continental Congress of the U. S. and the several colonies. Phila. 1872. 4° 8 facsimiles. h-f mor. by Bradstreet.

2341 The same. Descriptive catalogue of Confederate money and bonds. Phila. 1876. 4° large paper copy. h-f mor.

2342 HAWKINS, Edward. The silver coins of England. London. 1841. 8° 47 pls.

2343 The same. Description of the Anglo-Gallic coins in the British Museum. London. 1826. 4° 9 pls.

2344 HARDEN, Rev. H. E. A brief history of the soldiers' medals issued by the State of West Virginia. Wilkes-Barre. 1881. 8° 1 photo pl. Rare.

2345 HAYM, Nicholas. The British Treasury: containing Greek and Roman Medals of all sorts. London, 1719. 20. 2 vols. 4° num. pls h'f mor. by Bradstreet.

2346 The same work, in Italian. 2 vols. 4° uniform in binding with preceding No.

2347 HEATH'S (L.) Greatly improved infallible Government Counterfeit detector. Second edition, Boston, n. d. 16° 17 pls

2348 The same. Same work, banking-house edition. Boston. n. d. 4° 12 pls

2349 HEBREW customs; or, the missionary's return. Phila., 1834. 24° Jewish coins. p 87.

2350 HENN, Fred. Exchange tables, showing the value of U. S. currency in British sterling. N. Y., 1845. 8°

2351 HENFREY, H. W. A guide to the study and arrangement of English coins. London, 1870. 8° ills

2352 The same. Numismata Cromwelliana, or medallic history of Oliver Cromwell. London, 1873–75. 4° 8 pls In parts, as issued, complete.

2353 HENRY, J. Silver coins issued in England since the Conquest, with their values. London. 1877. 16° illus.

2354 The same. The series of English coins in copper, tin and bronze. London. 1879. 4°.

2355 HICKCOX, John H. A history of the bills of credit on paper money issued by New York. Albany, 1866. 8° h'f mor. by Bradstreet.

2356 The same. Same. Large paper copy, h'f mor.

2357 The same. An historical account of American coinage. N. Y., 1858. 4° 5 pls h'f mor., large paper copy, uniform in binding and size with preceding No. Very scarce.

2358 HIRSCH, J. C. Bibliotheca numismatica. Norimbergae. 1760. f° vellum.

2359 HISTORY of the Great Western Sanitary Fair. Cincinnati, 1864. 8° Coins and medals exhibited.

2360 HOBLER, Francis. Records of Roman History from Cneius Pompeius to Tiberius Constantinus, as exhibited on the Roman coins. Westminster, 1860. 2 vols. 4° ills.

2361 HODGES & Co. Manual de monedas de plata y oro. Contiene mayor numero de fac-similes de monedas de oro y plata que ninguna otra publicacion del mundo. N. Y. n. d. 8° h'f mor. num. ills.

2362 HOLLAND, H. W. Lincoln medals. Boston, 1875. 4°
Very scarce.

2363 HOMANS, I. Smith, Jr. The coin book. Phila., 1872.
8° 16 pls.

2364 HOMES, Henry A. Observations on the design and im-
port of medals. Albany, 1863. 8° h'f mor.

2365 HOTTON, F. B. Washingtoniana, or memorials of the
death of George Washington . . . with a catalogue of
medals commemorating the event. Roxbury, Mass.,
1865. 2 vols. 4° pls h'f mor. by Bradstreet. Large
paper copy.

2366 HUGHAN, W. J. A numerical and numismatical register
of lodges special and centenary medals, historical and numismatical sketches. London, 1878. 4°
5 colored plates.

2367 HUME's History of England. Student's edition. N. Y.,
1859. 8° num. ills. of coins and medals.

2368 HUMPHREYS, Henry Noel. The gold, silver, and copper coins of England, exhibited in a series of fac-
similes of the most interesting coins, printed in gold,
silver, and copper. Sixth edition. London, 1849.
12° h'f mor. by Bradstreet. 24 pls

2369 The Same. In original binding.

2370 The same. Ancient coins and medals. Illustrated by
numerous facsimile examples in actual relief, and in
the metals of the respective coins. London, 1850. 4°
16 pls In original binding, in perfect condition.

2371 The same. The coin collector's manual. London, 1853.
2 vols. 8° 11 pls

2372 The same. The coinage of the British Empire. Illustrated by facsimiles of the coins of each period,
worked in gold, silver, and copper. London, 1868.
4° 26 pls

2373 JACKSON, Samuel. An authentick account of the
weights, measures, etc., made use of at the several
parts of the East Indies, together with an account of
the different coins by which all accounts in Asia are
kept. London, 1764. 4°

2374 JACOB, Wm. An historical inquiry into the production
and consumption of the precious metals. London,
1831. 2 vols. 8° h'f calf.

2375 The same. American edition. Philadelphia, 1839.
1 vol. 8°.

2376 JEFFERY, F. J. Numismatic history of England. Liverpool, printed for private circulation, 1867. 8° 3 pls h'f mor.

2377 JENNINGS, David. An introduction to the knowledge of medals. Second edition. Birmingham, 1775. 12°

2378 JEWITT, L. Handbook of English coins. London, n.d. 24° 10 pls

2379 The same. Half-hours among some English antiquities. London, 1877. 12° Among coins, pp. 137–149, num. ills.

2380 [JOBERT.] La science des médailles antiques et modernes. Nouvelle edition. Amsterdam, 1717. 16° pls h'f mor. by Bradstreet.

2381 The same, in Italian. Venezia, 1728. 16° pls h'f mor? by Bradstreet.

2382 JOHNSON, Edwin L. J. A. Bolen's medals, cards and fac-similes. Springfield, 1882. 8°.

2383 JOHNSTON, E. B. A visit to the cabinet of the U. S. mint at Phila. Phila., 1876. 12° ills Scarce.

2384 JONES, G. F. The coin collector's manual. Philad'a, 1860. 4°

2385 KING, C. W. The natural history of precious stones and of the precious metals. London, 1870. 12° pls

2386 KOHLER, J. D. Historischer münz-belustigung. Nurnberg. 1729–1749. 21 vols. in 12. sm. 4° vellum. Num. illustrations, and a valuable work.

2387 LACHMANN, Dr. A. Neueste münzkunde. Abbildung und beschreibung der jetzt coursirenden gold-und silbermünzen. Leipzig, 1853. 2 vols. 8° 90 pls in relief.

2388 The same. New edition. Leipzig, 1867. 1 vol. 90 pls

2389 LANGDON, W. B. A descriptive catalogue of the Chinese collection now exhibited at St. George's Place. London, 1843. 8° Coins, p. 150.

2390 LANGLUME, J. Tableau des monnaies d'or et d'argent des principaux états du monde. 3d edition. Paris, n. d. sm. 4° num. pls h'f mor.

2391 LASKEY, J. C. A description of the series of medals struck at the national medal mint by order of Napoleon Bonaparte. London, 1818. 8° portrait.

2392 Another copy; same style.

2393 Another copy on large paper, mor. gilt edges.

2394 LAWRENCE & CO. Book of Coins. Illustrated. N. Y.,
1859. 4° paper cover, 36 p. Rare.

2395 LEAKE, S. M. An historical account of English money.
Third edition. London, 1793. 8° num. pts.

2396 LE CLERC, Jean. Histoire des Provinces-Unies des
Pays Bas . . . Avec les principales médailles et leur
explication. Amsterdam, 1728. 3 vols. 1° maps
and num. illus. Large paper copy.

2397 LEHR, Ernest. Les écus de cinq francs au point de vue
de la numismatique et de l'histoire. Avec 10 planches
en relief. Paris, 1870. 8° History of five-franc
pieces.

2398 LE POIS, A. Discours sur les medailles et gravures
antiques, principalement Romaines. Paris, par Mamert
Patisson, 1579. 4° Numerous plates, including one
of Priapus, usually torn out.

2399 LIBERAL Freemason. No. 6 of Vol. IV, p 175. Masonic
medals.

2400 LIDDELL, H. G. A history of Rome. New York, 1872.
12° num. ills of coins.

2401 LINDERMAN, H. R. Money and legal tender in the
U. S. New York, 1877. 12°

2402 LINDSAY, John. Notices of remarkable mediaeval coins,
mostly unpublished. Cork, 1849. 4° 3 pls.

2403 The same. A view of the history and coinage of the
Parthians. Cork, 1852. 4° 12 pls.

2404 LONG ISLAND Historical Society. First, second, third,
fourth, fifth, and sixth annual reports. Brooklyn,
1864–69. 3 vols. h'f mor.

2405 LONGSTAFFE, W. H. D. On the distinctions between
the pennies of Henry IV, V, and VI. no title page.

2406 LOON, G. van. Beschryving der Nederlandsche Histori-
penningen. 's Graavenhaage, 1723–31. 4 vols. 1°
vellum; num. plates and a rare and valuable work.

2407 LOWNDES, Wm. A report containing an essay for the
amendment of the silver coins. London, 1695. 12°
h'f mor. by Bradstreet.

2408 MACAULEY. Lays of Ancient Rome. Phila., 1858.
4° mor. num. ills. of coins

2409 MACOY, Robt. General history, cyclopedia and dictionary of Freemasonry. N. Y. 1868. 8° num. ills.

2410 MADDEN, F. W. The handbook of Roman numismatics.
London, 1861. 16° 5 pls

2411 The same. History of Jewish coinage. London, 1864. 8° 254 woodcuts.

2412 MANBY, G. W. Anastatic drawings of gold and silver medals presented by sovereigns and public bodies to Capt. Geo. Wm. Manby. Yarmouth, 1851. 8° portrait, 12 pls

2413 MARIS, Ed., Dr. Varieties of the copper issues of the U. S. mint in the year 1794. Phila., 1869. 12°

2414 The same. An historical sketch of the coins of New Jersey. Phila., 1881. f° folding phototype plate.

2415 MARSHALL, Geo. A view of the silver coin and coinage of Great Britain. London, 1838. 8° h'f mor.

2416 MASON's Coin and Stamp Collector's Magazine. Phila., 1867-72. Vols. I to VI complete. 8° h'f mor.

2417 MASONIC JEWEL. Nos. 9 & 11 of Vol. VI. The Penny of the Mark Master, p. 262. The half shekel of silver, p. 321.

2418 MASSACHUSETTS State Record and year book, 1847. Boston, 1847. 12° Massachusetts currency, p 210.

2419 MATHEWS, G. D. Our colonial coins. *In* St. Nicholas. No. 11, Vol. III. h'f mor. 30 ills.

2420 The same. The coinages of the world : ancient and modern. N. Y., 1876. 8° num. ills.

2421 MAYER, Lewis. Catalogue of the manuscripts, maps, medals, coins [etc.] of the Maryland Historical Societ. Baltimore, 1854. 8°

2422 MEDAILLE de la Garde Bourgeoise de Bruxelles en 1815. Bruxelles, 1869. 8° 1 pl

2423 MEDAILLES sur les principaux événements du règne de Louis le Grand. Baden, 1705. f° num. ills.

2424 MENESTRIER, C. F. Histoire du roy Louis le Grand par les médailles, etc. Paris, 1691. f° num. pls

4425 MERCER, Robt. W. The numismatic directory for 1881. Cincinnati, 1881 8°

2426 MERCHANT's and Banker's Almanac ; and Report of Finances, various dates. 12 vols. 8°

2427 MERZDORF, J. F. L. Th. Die denkmünzen der Freimaurerbrüderschaft. Oldenburg, 1851. 8° 1 pl

2428 METALLIC money, its value, and its functions. Phila., 1841 8° h'f mor.

2429 METROPOLITAN COIN BOOK, illustrated. N. Y., 1860. 4° paper cover. Rare.

2430 MEXICAN WAR. Reports of committees to prepare and present medals to the N. Y. Regiment of Volunteers. etc. N. Y., 1859. 8°

2431 MICHELS, I. C. The current gold and silver coins of all nations. Phila., 1886. 1° num. ills.

2432 MICKLEY, J. J. Dates of U. S. coins and their degrees of rarity. Phila., 1858. 8°

2433 MILLER, M. T. The Coins of the world. Phila., 1849. 12°. 12 pls h'f mor., by Bradstreet. Rare.

2434 MILLIN, A. L. Medallic history of Napoleon. Supplement. London, 1821. 4° h'f mor. 14 pls

2435 MILLINGEN, J. Ancient coins of Greek cities and kings. London, 1831. 4° h'f mor. 5 pls

2436 MORRIS, Robt. Ancient coins found in Holy Soil. *In* Our Monthly. Vol. II. h'f mor.

2437 The same. Medals of the Freemasons. *In* The Am. Quarterly Review of Freemasonry. Vol. II. h'f mor.

2438 The same. Freemasonry in the Holy Land. N. Y., 1872. 8° ills. of coins. etc.

2439 MUDIE, James. An historical and critical account of a grand series of National medals. London, 1820. 4° h'f mor. num. pls

2440 Another copy. h'f calf.

2441 MURRAY, John. The truth of Revelation demonstrated by an appeal to existing monuments, sculptures, gems, coins and medals. London, 1840. 8° 5 pls of coins. etc.

2442 **N**AHUYS. Histoire numismatique du royaume de Hollande. sous le règne de S. M. Louis-Napoleon. Amsterdam, 1858. 4° 14 pls

2443 Napoleon III. History of Julius Cæsar. London, n. d. 2 vols. 8° Notes on the ancient coins collected in the excavations at Alise. Vol. II. p 582.

2444 NEWCOMB, J. C. Catalogue of an exceedingly interesting and valuable collection of silver medals of all nations. To be sold at auction. May 25-27, 1870. 8° 8 photo plates. h'f calf.

2445 NEW ENGLAND Historical Genealogical Society. Proceedings. January, 1872. Boston, 1872. 8° The Sears medal. p. 23.

2446 NEW YORK State Library. Catalogues. 1846, 1850, 1855, 1856. 6 vols. 8° Volume of 1856 contains medals. etc.

2447 NIBOYET. P Les rois de France. Avec les empreintes
des monnaies appartement aux divers règnes. Leipsic,
1854. 8° 11 pls

2448 NICHOLS. T. A handy-book of the British Museum.
London. 1870. 8° ills. Coins and medals, p. 384.

2449 NICOLAS, Sir Nicholas Harris. History of the Orders
of Knighthood of the British Empire : of the order of
the Guelphs of Hanover ; and of the medals, clasps,
and crosses conferred for naval and military services.
London, 1842. 4 vols. large 4° num. beautifully
colored plates of orders, medals, etc.

2450 NOBLE, Mark. Two dissertations upon the mint and
coins of the episcopal-palatines of Durham. Birmingham, 1780. 4° ills.

2451 O'CALLAGHAN, E. B. Documentary history of the
State of N. Y. Albany, 1850. 4 vols. 4° Medals
and coins, III, 715, 3 pls

2450 The same. Medals and coins of N.Y. no title. 12° 3 pls
Rare.

2453 ORDWAY, N. G. The American Bond detector : also
plates of existing coins. Washington, 1869. oblong
4° numerous plates.

2454 OUTLINES of Roman history. Phila., 1846. 24° num.
ills. of Roman coins.

2455 PAINE, N. Remarks on the early paper currency of
Massachusetts. Cambridge, 1866. 8° ills. h'f mor.

2456 PATIN. C. Introductio ad Historiam nummismatum.
Amstelaedami. 1683. 24° ills.

2457 The same Thesaurus numismatum antiquorum & re
centiorum ex auro, argento, & aere ab illustriss &
Excellentiss. D. D. Pietro Mauroceno. Veneliis,
1783. 4° num. ills.

2458 The same. Thesaurus numismatum e musaeo Caroli
Patini. [Paris.] Sumptibus Autoris, 1672. 4° num.
ills.

2459 PEDRUSI. (Paolo). I Cesari in oro, argento, medaglioni
e metallo grande . . . raccolti nel Farnese Museo,
Parma, 1694. 7 vols. f° num. pls full mor., gilt
edges.

2460 PEGGE. S. An Essay on the coins of Cunobelin. London,
1766. 4° 2 pls. h'f mor.

2461 The same. An assemblage of coins fabricated by authority of the Archbishop of Canterbury. London. 1772. 4° portrait and plate. h'f mor. by Bradstreet.

2462 Penny Magazine. 1836. London. 4° English coins. pp 275, etc.

2463 Percival, W. The universal library of literature, and illustrated mirror of the world. Philadelphia, 1860. 4° num. ills

2464 Peters, J. R. Miscellaneous remarks upon the government, history, etc., of the Chinese. New York, 1845. 8° h'f mor. Coins, etc., pp 84, 101-3.

2465 Pettigrew, T. J. On superstitions connected with medicine and surgery. Phila., 1844. 12° Royal touch pieces. 1 pl and p 162. Rare.

2466 Pettingal, John. A dissertation upon the Tascia, or legend on the British coins of Cunobelin and others. London, 1763. 4° 1 pl

2467 Peyton, G. How to detect counterfeit bank notes. N. Y., 1856. 8° 4 pls

2468 Phelps, N. A. History of Simsbury, Granby, and Canton, from 1642 to 1845. Hartford, 1845. 8° h'f mor. Higley's coppers, p 118. Rare.

2469 Phelps, R. N. A history of Newgate of Connecticut. Albany, 1860. 4° portrait. Granby coppers, p 15.

2470 Philadelphia Library Company Catalogue of books. Phila. 1807. 8° Coins, pp 534-600.

2471 Phillips, Henry, Jr. An historical sketch of the paper money issued by Pennsylvania. Phila., 1862. 8°

2472 The same. Same. Bound in h'f mor.

2473 The same. Worship of the Sun. The story told by a coin of Constantine the Great. Phila. 1884. 4° Rare.

2474 The same. Notes upon the collection of coins and medals now upon exhibition at the Pennsylvania Museum. Philadelphia, 1879. 2 vols

2475 The same. Remarks upon a coin of Smyrna. Philadelphia, 1882. 8°

2476 The same. A catalogue of the New Jersey bills of credit. Philadelphia, 1865. 8° h'f mor.

2477 The same. The pleasures of numismatic science. Philadelphia, 1867. 8° h'f mor.

2478 The same. Historical sketches of the paper currency of the American Colonies. First and second series. Roxbury, 1865-66. 2 vols. 4° h'f mor.

2479 [PICKETT, J. T]. Sigillogia. Being some account of the great or broad seal of the Confederate States of America. Washington, 1873. 8° h'f mor.

2480 PINKERTON, John. An essay on medals. London. 1874. 12° h'f calf.

2481 The same. Third edition. London, 1808. 2 vols, 8° num. pls h'f mor. by Bradstreet.

2482 POOLE, R. S. Numismatics. From Encyclopedia Britannica. 4°

2483 POOLE, S. L. Catalogue of Oriental coins in the British Museum. Vols. I. II. and III. London, 1875–1877. 3 vols. 8° numerous autotype pls

2484 The same. Catalogue of the collection of Oriental coins belonging to Col. C. S. Guthrie. I. Coins of the Awawi Khalifehs. Hertford, 1874. 8° 5 autotype pls

2485 POSTE, B. A vindication of the Celtic inscriptions on Gaulish and British coins. London, 1862. 8° ills.

2486 POWNALL, Rev. A. The Royal bust on early groats.— New type of the first Ethelstan.—Find of 15th century groats. London, v. d. 8° 3 vols.

2487 PRIME, W. C. Coins, medals, and seals, ancient and modern. New York, 1861. 4° num. pls

2488 The same. Coins and coinage. Coins in America. Ills. *In* Harper's monthly, 1860. h'f mor.

2489 PYTHAGORAS Lodge in Brooklyn. Catalogue of books and medals. N. Y. 1859. 8° Very scarce.

2490 RAFFLES, Sir T. S. The history of Java. London, 1830. 2 vols. 8°, and atlas of plates, f°, containing pl (87) of ancient coins.

2491 RAPIN. History of England. London, 1743. 2 vols. f° num. ills. of coins.

2492 REID, H. First lessons in Arithmetic. London, 1853. 8° English coins, illus.. p 49.

2493 RIDDELL, J. L. A monograph of the silver dollar, good and bad. New Orleans, 1845. 8° num. ills. Rare.

2494 ROBERTSON. J. D. A handbook to the coinage of Scotland. London, 1878. small 4° ills

2495 ROMAN antiquities. No title page. 12° pls of coins, etc

2496 ROUGH, T. de. Den Nederlandschen Herauld, ofte tractaet van wapenen. Numerous ills. of orders. coats of arms, etc.

2497 REDING, R. Annals of the coinage of Great Britain and its dependencies. Third edition. London. 1840. 5 vols. 4° num. pls. h'f mor. Last and best edition; in extra fine condition, and a very valuable work.

2498 SAINSBURY, John. The Napoleon Museum. The history of France illustrated from Louis XIV to the end of the reign and death of the Emperor. Comprising marbles, bronzes, . . medallions . . . . coins, medals, etc. London. 1845. large 4° 40 pls of facsimiles, etc.

2499 SANDHAM, A. Coins, tokens and medals of the Dominion of Canada, with supplement. Montreal. 1869. 1872. 2 vols. 8° num. ills. h'f mor. by Bradstreet. Very scarce.

2500 The same. Medals commemorative of the visit of H.R.H. the Prince of Wales to Montreal in 1860. Montreal. 1871. 8° photo pls

2501 The same. McGill College and its medals. Montreal 1872. 8° photo plates, h'f mor, by Bradstreet.

2502 SATTERLEE, A. H. An arrangement of medals and tokens struck in honor of the Presidents of the U. S. New York, 1862. 8° h'f mor. Very scarce.

2503 SCHLUMBERGER, G. Les principautés françaises du Levant d'après les plus récents découvertes de la numismatique. Paris. 1877. 8° ills

2504 SCHUBERT, F. F. de. Monnayes Russes des derniers trois siècles. Leipsic, 1857. text, 4° h'f mor; atlas, obl. 4° 37 pls in relief. A beautiful and rare work.

2505 SCHUM, F. Les rois fédéraux de la Suisse et leurs médailles. Bruxelles. 1858. 8° 5 pls.

2506 SHARPE, S. The history of Egypt under the Ptolemies. London. 1838. 8° num. references to coins.

2507 The same. Texts from the Holy Bible explained by the help of the ancient monuments. London. 1869. 12° num. ills. of coins.

2508 SIMON, J. An essay towards an historical account of Irish coins. Dublin. 1810. 4° num. pls. h'f mor. Best edition.

2509 SIMON, J. A list of the Lancashire script of tradesmen's tokens and town pieces of the 17th century. London. 1872. 8° pls.

2510 SKELTON, H. P. New illustrated manual of the copper, gold and silver coins of all modern nations. London. n. d. 2 pts in vol. 28 pls in relief. h'f calf

2511 SLAFTER, E. F.   The Vermont coinage.   Montpelier,
Vt., 1870.   8°   Only 50 copies printed.

2512 SMILEY, T. T.   Scripture Geography.   Phila., 1834.
12° Maps and num. illus. of coins.

2513 SMITH, A. M.   Coins and Coinage.   The U. S. Mint.
Rare pieces of gold, silver, nickel, copper, brass.
Money, tokens, medals, etc. fully described and
market price quoted.   Phila., 1881.   12° num. illus.

2514 SMITH, Rev. J. J.   Numismata Collegii de Gonvile et
Caius.   Cambridge, 1846.   4°.

2515 SMITH, WM.   A classical dictionary of biography, mythology and geography.   London, 1869.   8° num. ills. of
coins.

2516 The same.   A history of Greece.   New York, 1872.   8°
num. ills. of coins.

2517 The same.   A smaller history of Greece.   New York,
n. d.   16° illus. of coins.

2518 SMYTH, Wm. H.   Descriptive catalogue of a cabinet of
Roman Imperial large brass medals.   Bedford, 1834.   4°

2519 The same.   Descriptive catalogue of a cabinet of Roman
family coins.   London, 1856.   4°

2520 SNELLING, T.   A view of the silver coin and coinage of
England.——A view of the gold coin and coinage of
England.   London, 1762–63.   2 vols. f° num. pls.

2521 The same.   A view of the coins at this time current
throughout Europe.   London, 1766.   16° 24 pls

2522 The same.   Seventy-one plates of gold and silver coin.
London, n. d.   8°

2523 SNOWDEN, J. R.   The medallic memorials of Washington in the mint of the U. S.   Phila., 1861.   4° 22 pls

2524 The same.   A description of ancient and modern coins
in the cabinet collection at the mint of the U. S.
Phila., 1861.   4° 22 pls

2525 The same.   The coins of the Bible, and its money terms.
Philadelphia.   n. d.   24° ills.

2526 The same.   International Coinage.   (From Lippincott's
Magazine for January, 1870.)   h'f mor.

2527 STOUT. J. V.   Table of the intrinsic value of the current
money of every nation.   8° Folding plate, h'f mor.

2528 STROBRIDGE, W. H.   Antiquity of Money.   In The
Old Curiosity Shop.   No. 3, Vol. I.   h'f mor.

2529 STUKELEY, W.   The medallic history of Carausius,
Emperor in Britain.   London, 1757.   2 pts in 1 vol.
4° num. pls   h'f mor. by Bradstreet.

2530 SUMNER, W. G. A history of American currency. New York, 1874. 8

2531 SYMSON, Wm. An essay on weighing of gold, etc., wherein is shewn an effectual method for discovering and detecting of counterfeit pieces of money. London, 1756. 12° h f mor. by Bradstreet.

2532 THOMAS, E. The Initial coinage of Bengal. Hertford, 1866–73. 2 vols. 8° h f mor. pls

2533 The same. Comments on recent Pehlvi decipherments and contributions to the early history and geography of Tabaristan illustrated by coins. London, 1872. 8° 2 pls

2534 The same. Early Sassanian inscriptions, seals, and coins. London, 1868. 8° pls

2535 The same. On the coins of the Patan Sultans of Hindustan. London, 1847. 8° pls

2536 TILL, W. Descriptive particulars of English coronation medals. London, 1888. 12° 2 pls.

2537 The same. An essay on the Roman denarius and English silver penny. London, 1837. 12° ills.

2538 TOUSSENEL, T. Precis chronologique de l'Histoire de France pour servir de texte explicatif aux planches gravées sur acier par le procédé Collas d'après la collection des médailles historiques des rois de France. Paris, 1844. 4° 8 pls.

2539 VAILLANT, Jean Foy. Numismata Imperatorum Romanorum praestantiora a Julius Caesare ad Postumum usque. Romae, 1794. 3 vols. f° num. illus. calf, gilt edges. Fourth and best edition in perfect condition; a rare and valuable work.

2540 The same. Lutetiae Parisiorum. 1696. 2 vols. in 1. 4° vellum.

2541 VAUX, W. S. W. On coins of Marathas, and of Kananeskires and Auzaze. Reprinted from Numismatic Chronicle. 8° 4 pl

2542 VICO, E. Discorsi di M. Enea Vico sopra le medaglie de gli antichi. Vinegia, 1668. Small 4° Portrait of Cosmo de Medici.

2543 VOOGT, W. J. de. Geschiedenis van het muntwezen der verenigde Nederlanden. Amsterdam, 1874. 4° h f calf.

2544 VRIES, J. de. Nederlandische Gedenkpenningen. 's Graavenhage, 1829-37. 2 vols 4° 12 pls.

2545 WASSERMAN. Catalogue of the Royal Museum at Berlin. Berlin, 1869. 16° Coins, p 34.

2546 WEBSTER, W. List of unedited Greek Coins. London, 1873. 8°. Reprinted from Numismatic Chronicle.

2547 WELLS, E. Sacred Geography. Charleston, 1817. 4 num. plates of coins. Rare.

2548 WHELAN, P. The numismatic atlas of the Roman Empire. London, 1864. 8°

2549 WHITNEY, J. D. The metallic wealth of the U. S. Phila., 1854. 8°

2550 WILL, G. A. Der Nürnbergischen münz-belustigungen. Nürnberg, 1764-67. 4 vols. sm 4° Complete.

2551 WILLIS, G. Current notes. A series of articles on antiquities, etc. London, 1825-55. 2 vols sm 4°.

2552 WILSON, T. An Archaeological Dictionary. London, 1793. 8°

2553 WINES, E. C. A Peep at China. Phila, 1839. 8° h'f mor. Coins, p 48.

2554 WOODWARD, A. Wampum. Second edition. Albany, 1880. 8°

2555 WOODWARD W. Elliot. Washington memorial medals; privately printed, 1865. 8°. English drawing paper (12 printed) paper cover 16 pp

2556 WOODWORTH, J. Reminiscences of Troy. Albany, 1860. sm. 4° Coins, etc., p 75.

2557 WYATT, T. History of the Kings of France. Phila., 1846. 12° num. pls of medals.

2558 The same. Memoirs of the Generals, Commodores, and other Commanders in the American Army and Navy, and who were presented with medals. Phila., 1848. 8° 82 ills. of medals. h'f calf.

2559 ZABRISKIE, A. C. A descriptive catalogue of the Political and Memorial Medals struck in honor of Abraham Lincoln. New York, 1873. 8° h'f mor. Very scarce.

2560 ZACHARIAS, E. Numotheca Numismatica Latomorum. Dresden, 1840-5 8 parts in 1 vol., num pls. Rare and earliest work on Masonic Medals.

2561 Coin Box 14½ x 14½ in. Cover on hinges and opens like a book. 122 compartments nearly 1½ in. deep : suitable for a collection of half dollars, cents, etc., or of postage stamps; cherry wood ; condition very good.

3662 An elegant ornamental coin and medal cabinet of solid rosewood, mounted on a solid rosewood table, forming a beautiful and useful article of furniture for drawing room or library. The table, also of solid rosewood, is 2 ft. 6 in. long, 3 ft. wide, and 1 ft. 9 in. deep. The exterior dimensions of the cabinet proper are 3 ft. 10 in. in height by 2 ft. in width and 14 in. in depth; it is handsomely carved above and fitted with two handsome ornaments, eight inches in height. There are 68 drawers numbered on boxwood knobs; interior dimensions of each 10½ by 10 in. varying in depth; velvet lined, many furnished with movable partitions, double glass doors and two extra deep drawers above. Very handsome and perfect; originally the property of Dr. Mackenzie, who had it made to order at a very high price.